THE MAGIC OF MG

The M.G. image in the thirties.
Bryan de Grineau's drawing of Tazio Nuvolari winning the 1933 Ulster T.T.

THE MAGIC OF MG

Mike Allison

DALTON WATSON LTD
LONDON

First Published 1972

ISBN 0 901564 095
Library of Congress Catalog Card Number 72-88716

Process Engravings by Star Illustration Works Ltd

Printed in England by the Lavenham Press Ltd
for the publishers
DALTON WATSON LTD
76 Wardour Street London W1V 4AN

Distributed in the USA by
Motorbooks International
3501 Hennepin Avenue South
Minneapolis
Minnesota 55408

Preface

If any member of the British public is asked to name a sports car manufacturer, the chances are that he will name M.G. The products of the little factory at Abingdon-on-Thames, some seven miles south of Oxford, and sports cars generally have been synonymous for over forty years.

Public imagination was probably initially aroused when an M.G. became the first 'baby' car to exceed 100 mph, in 1930. During the next five years the exploits of M.G. in the 750cc and 1100cc classes of motor sport became known throughout Europe as of the highest order. An M.G. became the first 1100cc car to exceed 200 mph in 1939.

Since this time M.G. cars have been successful in sports car racing and record breaking, but far more significant has been the fact that from 1948 M.G. cars started a cult, particularly in the U.S.A., for the British Sports Car, which has resulted in the production of M.G. rising to quite unprecedented levels.

In spite of this, many writers of self presumed motoring wisdom have sought to denigrate the success and performance of M.G's, to prove that this or that car gives better performance or handling, and to show that the competition models were something "extra-special" and not related to the car you buy. One can only assume that the public do not regard these people and their opinions highly!

Certainly the adjective "Magic" has been applied to two very successful cars, but there was nothing particularly unusual in the mechanical specifications of these, nor was a spell or wand used in their preparation! And yet magic is a word which can be applied to M.G. cars with some justification, for the cars themselves do generate an enthusiasm amongst owners which is unparalleled by another relatively large production *marque.*

The M.G. Car Club bears testimony to this fact, being easily the largest one-make sporting club providing meetings for its members: what other club can organise a race meeting for members only, in which 140 out of 160 entrants are driving a single make car?

What then is this M.G. "Magic", which is liked by so many, and yet not appreciated by even more?

Personally, I was first affected by the Magic during the Second World War, when as a small boy, the radiator of what must have been a P-type could be seen in a neighbour's garage. The first M.G. I rode in was an SA saloon, owned by a school teacher, but it was my own first P-type which really set the enthusiasm alight. Since this time, I have owned a wide variety of M.G's, and driven many more. It should not be thought however that I have not experienced the delights of other makes, but unlike these sometimes more pretentious motor cars there have been few M.G. sports cars which I have not found pleasant to drive.

True, I have driven some poor examples, but the vast majority of these have been mechanically neglected examples, or modified cars in which owners have sought to 'improve' performance. On the other hand it should not be thought that I do not think there are any basically bad M.G's, but the fact remains that taken in context of their time, M.G. cars have offered high standards of performance, steering, brakes and roadholding, better than most and at least equal to many supposedly better.

Although a sports car must stand by its performance, it is a fact that this is not necessarily the only feature which will sell cars. A vehicle must not only go well, it must also *look* right. Perhaps this one feature has contributed as much to the success of M.G. as anything — there have been very few ugly M.G's, and those which were did not sell in large numbers.

M.G's display a simplicity of line which is difficult to improve, a fact about which there is little dissention and probably contributes more to M.G. magic than any other single feature. The cars *look* right, and that which looks right generally *is* so.

What this book sets out to show is this simplicity of line which has followed from model to model, improving perhaps year by year, and at the same time indicating something of performance.

The photographs have been chosen from several thousand, and although some are well-known, no apology is made for including these if they serve the purpose intended. Most of them appear exactly as they print from the negatives, they are not retouched since it was felt that a faithful record of the cars was of more use than pictures of what we would like to see!

The text is not a history but a mixture of fact and personal opinion, but I have attempted to restrict the latter to comments on styling and handling only although remaining aware of the fact that these items vary from person to person. More important I have restricted the written word to an absolute minimum in order to give space to as many photographs as possible, since the need for such a book has become apparent from the number of people who have asked for copies of pictures from the M.G. Car Club files. It is hoped that in addition to these people, more will be affected by the Magic of M.G. and perhaps try the cars for themselves rather than believe the writings of others.

M.A.

Contents

Acknowledgment

It would be impossible to name everyone who has contributed to the production of this book, and those named below are those whom the author and publishers can best remember. If there are others who should have been mentioned, we apologise, and offer thanks, most particularly to the photographers whose work we have not been able to identify.

The author and publishers would like to record their sincere appreciation to the following persons and organisations for their help with material and photographs and for their permission to reproduce them.

To Alan Zafer of the British Leyland Motor Corporation, who gave his blessing to its production, to the M.G. Car Club Limited, who provided the greater part of the material used, and to the International Publishing Corporation who gave permission for the use of their copyright photographs.

In addition the author would like to thank the following people for supplying photographs from their personal collections: Piers Hubbard, Gordon Cobban, Philip Bayne-Powell, the late Sam Nash, John Lewis, Mike Garton, Syd Beer, and Steve Dear.

Denis Lowe and Charles Carter of British Leyland gave a great deal of time, encouragement and advice in the selection of photographs, and the last named actually located the negatives from the archives.

So far as the text is concerned it is a compilation of information from various sources, particularly the M.G. Car Club records and thanks must go especially to Reg Jackson, Alec Hounslow and Henry Stone for retelling their experiences during the racing days, to Tom Viner, Bill Lane, Cecil Cousins and to John and Gracie Lewis for helping with information relating to the early days. John Knight and Roy Brocklehurst helped with details from more recent times, and Terry Hemmings and John Bibbing filled in recent production data.

Particular thanks are due to Wilson McComb, in whose department I worked for nearly two years and during which time he inspired me with the need to differentiate between personal opinion and recorded fact. To Gordon Cobban and Margaret O'Brien go sincere thanks for allowing me to visit the Club Office and search out information at all sorts of odd times.

Lastly most especial thanks are due to my wife Anne, who gave consistent encouragement, supplied coffee, typed the entire manuscript, and still puts up with my octagonal hobby, both theoretical and practical.

CHAPTER ONE

Oxford and Cowley

The first M.G. was not "Old Number One". M.G's identifiable as such were built for some two years before that famous car was built. It might, however, be true to say that Old Number One was the first M.G. built specifically for sporting purposes.

The early days of M.G. production showed a process of evolution rather than a decision to go into car building. For some years The Morris Garages of Oxford, who were, and are, the Morris Distributors for Oxfordshire had offered a wide range of special equipment for use on Morris cars.

In addition to this the firm became involved with the preparation of local motor cycles and motor cars for sporting purposes, chiefly in the inter-Varsity speed trials, so that it was inevitable that with customers of sporting instincts around, a tradition of motor sport would develop amongst the employees.

In 1922 Cecil Kimber became General Manager and the following year he drove a Morris Cowley fitted with a Morris Garages special "Chummy" body in the London – Lands End Trial, gaining a Gold Medal for making an unpenalised run. It was from these roots that the M.G. image developed.

The earliest M.G's as such were special bodied Morris Cowleys, similar to that driven by Kimber in the 1923 Lands End and were built during the winter of 1923/4. Modifications to the chassis were few: springs were flattened and the engines may have been tuned by polishing ports and balancing combustion chambers and carefully aligning ports. Very few of these cars were built, since Morris Motors introduced a similar Cowley Chummy at a considerably lower price!

The next M.G. was based on the larger engined Oxford chassis, although a number of Cowley features were standardised. Again springs were flattened, engines mildly tuned and beaded-edge tyres were used, but four-wheel brakes were adopted together with servo assistance. Bodywork was open four-seater finished in polished aluminium and although a range of special saloons was offered, these were apparently not regarded as "M.G's" at first. The earliest advertisements for M.G's, which displayed the now famous octagon, were first seen at this time.

However, it may not have been until the 1925 model year that M.G's went into serious production, and it was early in this year that "No. 1" was built from non-standard components.

A wider range of bodies was made available as demand was increased, including a two-seater, a four-seater, both open, and a sporting salonette which featured a boot politely described as a "duck's tail". Colour finish was two-tone, the open cars having upper parts and mudguards finished in claret or blue and the lower parts polished aluminium. The closed car had a genuine two-tone paint colour finish, and if not the first to use this striking colour effect M.G. were certainly early in the field. The result was quite breathtaking, for the cars looked low and "sporting", and the image of the M.G. cars was now set. A similar range of bodies was continued for the 1926 model year, and it was during this period that M.G. moved to a part of the old Osberton Radiators factory in the Banbury Road, Oxford, for their car production activities.

During 1926 the Morris Bullnose was replaced by what we now distinguish as the "flat nose". In addition to the radiator, the chassis was considerably revised which improved handling but unfortunately power outputs did not change and performance suffered with the extra weight penalties.

The M.G. versions followed similar lines to the earlier cars, but were of necessity wider, which made them slightly less attractive. The radiator began to take the shape of the now familiar style, and during 1927 the enamelled octagon badge appeared on the radiator for the first time, at first surrounded by a blue ring, with a nickel badge in the middle of the honeycomb and later in the now familiar cream and brown form. Body styling was helped by the introduction of "engine turned" lower panels in place of the polished aluminium. A lightweight Weymann-type fabric covered saloon was offered along with all the earlier styles. Balloon tyres were standardised on M.G's at this time. During 1927 the move to the first M.G. factory at Cowley took place.

For 1928 the model was called the M.G. 14/40 Mark IV Sports, and considerable discussion has resulted as to how the "Mark IV" part arose. Personally I think it arose because the car was in the fourth year of production, although the "14/40" is more difficult to understand and may have been a matter of alliteration. Various improvements were made, including the braking system, from which the Servo was *deleted.* One of the less attractive features was the use of myriads of octagons — a device which was to be the motif of M.G's until the demise of the TF. The side valve cars entered their final year of production in 1929 and none were built after the move to Abingdon the following year.

This model is one of the few M.G's which I have never driven, so that I can only judge their performance from second-hand opinions. It seems that the cars were pleasant to drive and capable of a reasonable acceleration to a touring gait of around 60 mph which could be maintained, thanks to good handling. The earlier cars are more sought after now, but the later ones were undoubtedly better with improved suspension, brakes and steering. In 1927 a 14 hp car was the first M.G. to win a race.

SPECIFICATION

Bore x Stroke	75 x 102 mm
Capacity	1802 cc
Valve operation	Side valves
Power output	Approximately 35 bhp
@ rpm	4000
Gearbox	3-speed non-synchromesh
Brakes	Mechanical or Perrot system, Servo assisted until 1928.
Drums (diameter)	12″
Number built	Approximately 1,300
Body Styles	2 seater open, 4 seater open, 2 door salonette, 4 door saloons of various types

It is debatable whether the Cowley Sports (Above) *was the inspiration for the M.G. — it certainly possesses many of the features which later characterised the marque.*

This was a very early Morris Garages body on an F-type Morris Oxford Six.

Not the first M.G., but the first sports car built in 1925 by Kimber — "Old No. 1".

A 1925 production four-seater, with the upper parts coloured either claret or blue and lower panels polished.

Examples of the 1924 production four-seater — polished alloy coachwork resplendent.

The 1925 two-seater. In the lower photograph the octagon motifs can be seen on the sill nameplates. The instrument layout is well scattered, but hardly ergonomic!

A 1926 Salonette, with tail, pictured at a 1969 M.G. Car Club meeting. Apart from the radiator badge, it is very original.

For 1927 the flat radiator was adopted, and lower coach panels were engine-turned instead of polished. CA 9711 was a road test car. Instruments are better grouped.

The four-seater was actually quite handsome. The M.G. number plate was a fake, but these were later sold by University Motors on M.G.'s for a premium.

The two-door salonette for 1927 was two-tone coloured, and well appointed. The model in the later photograph is actress Madeleine Carroll.

The salonette with "ducks tail" continued. The selection of hand levers can be seen — the "gear lever" to the drivers right actually dipped the headlamps.

One of the earliest attempts to outdo M.G. at their own business! A Jarvis-bodied 14/40 of 1927 vintage.

The 1928 chassis and four-seater tourer.

Above and Left: *WL 3450 was a factory demonstrator — a 1927 fabric bodied saloon known as the "Old Speckled Hen".*
Below: *the panelled four-door 1928 saloon displays some of the style of the Riley "Monaco".*

1928 model saloons. Above: *4 door metal panelled Mark IV version.* Below: *2-door metal bodied and slightly earlier car, now in the Bressingham collection.*

A two-seater with dickey dating from early 1927.

The interior of the final form of the 14/40 — showing that octagons were much to the fore.

A rare Mark IV two-door salonette, with a dickey . . . . surely an inhumane banishment seat?

CHAPTER TWO

Vintage Splendour

The M.G. Six was first introduced at the 1928 Motor Show. The side-valve 14 h.p. cars were by this time in their fourth year, and it was fairly obvious to all that something new was needed if public interest in the new marque was to be maintained.

As related in the previous chapter, the 14/40 became the Mark IV and to accompany the latest variation not one but *two* brand new models appeared on the M.G. display to accompany it. These new models were at opposite ends of both price and size scale: the smaller we meet in the next chapter, the larger being the 18 h.p. M.G. Six.

During 1927 a Morris Light Six had been announced, powered by a 2½-litre 6 cylinder engine. What was unusual for this Morris was the fact that the camshaft was over the valves operating the latter through 'L' shaped rockers. This car did not reach production, and it was in the "Major" in which the unit was eventually used in a Morris, and subsequently in the "Isis". The unit was a natural for Kimber however, and it has been suggested that he was in collusion with the Morris engine designer, Frank Woolard.

The cylinder block and crankcase were cast in one, with a detachable head. A four main bearing counterbalanced crankshaft was featured, with chain and gear drive to the camshaft. This chain was deviated in its upward path to drive the distributor, oil pump, dynamo and water pump: all from a single skew gear shaft which contributed to various running problems. Silent running of the camshaft gears was ensured by the interposition of a fabroil wheel.

The inlet manifold was peculiar, in that it fed what was really a cross-flow port layout, but the carburettors were mounted low down on the cylinder block under the exhaust manifold, the inlet charge passing through the block and then up to the ports in the head.

The engine was however smooth running and very quiet, with very good torque characteristics. Maximum power was never officially quoted and the figures below were interpolated from a graph of unknown origin.

The chassis followed 14/40 practice, although of heavier construction, the axles being M.G. designed and carrying Perrot-type brake gear. Marles Steering was used. Early prototypes had 14/40 type bolt-on wheels but all production cars had Rudge-Whitworth type hubs which were fitted to all subsequent pre-war M.G.'s.

The radiator deserves special mention, for it was the crystallisation of the various types fitted to later 14 h.p. cars, and at the same time set the fashion which followed right through to 1953 and can still be seen in vestigial form on current models.

Coachwork was commodious and luxurious. The car was also reasonably priced, well below the luxury class and in direct competition with Alvis and Lagonda. 80 mph top speed was offered together with good roadholding, and general handling well ahead of its competitors. If it had a fault then the three speed gearbox could be cited, though the torque curve of the engine was such that this was no real handicap for touring.

For 1929 a new chassis was designed, of much heavier construction, with wider track, four speed gearbox and much improved cable operated brakes. This new confection became known as the 18/80 Mark II, the older model continuing as the Mark I. The Mark II started the first series of alphabetical chassis prefixes, and may be referred to as the A-type, though seldom is.

The Mark II carried bodywork of improved standards, although one or two variants were in fact of Mark I origin, using wider mudguards. The chassis gave more rigidity, which allowed the use of softer road springs, while the gearbox helped to compensate for additional weight. The Mark II was undoubtedly a better car than the Mark I, but it was on average £100 dearer model for model, so that the Mark I continued and outsold the later car.

During 1929 the Mark I was fitted with improved, cable operated, brakes and in 1930 a Speed Model was introduced which had a *guaranteed* 80 mph performance. The Mark II Speed Model was offered but the greater weight of the chassis detracted from the good acceleration for which the Mark I variant was praised.

The ultimate 18/80 was undoubtedly the Mark III, or B-type. Designed as a racing car in the Bentley tradition, and based on the Mark II chassis it featured many of the Mark II details. The engine was a modified form of the 18/80, but had a true cross-flow head for the first time on an M.G., and had dry sump lubrication. 100 bhp and 100 mph were hoped for, the former was never achieved, in spite of attention by Shell, and the latter was not available as a sustained speed. The model however became known as the 18/100 Mark III and variously called "Tiger", "Tigress" and "Tigresse".

The first competition outing of the car ended in disaster when the bearings ran during the 1930 Double Twelve race at Brooklands. The car was not run again by the Company, and subsequent competition appearances were few. Perhaps it was designed too late: the days of the large, so-called, vintage sports car type were numbered — eclipsed in terms of performance and value for money by the other smaller cars now appearing from Abingdon in large numbers.

Competition appearances by the 18 hp cars were not the prerogative of the Mark III however, for both Mark I and Mark II models appeared in rallies and trials. A Mark I was the first M.G. to compete in the Monte Carlo Rally, driven by Sir Francis Samuelson in 1929, he also ran a Mark II in the 1930 event. However, these cars were never spectacularly successful in competition, their *metier* being as a fast touring car. This they accomplished without doubt, maintaining and improving standards set by the earlier cars.

The Mark I was in production until early in 1931, while the Mark II was built until the following year, although new models were still available from stock until early in 1934. The fact that the 18/80 sold slowly was a reflection more of the depressed economy of the world than of the car, for it was one of the really good M.G.'s, whether regarded in relation to its period or in retrospect.

It set one standard which did not vary: that M.G. cars should represent good value for money.

SPECIFICATIONS

	Mark I	*Mark II*	*18/100 Mark III*
Bore x Stroke	69 x 110 mm	69 x 110 mm	69 x 110 mm
Valve operation	Single o/h camshaft	Single o/h camshaft	Single o/h camshaft
Capacity	2468 cc	2468 cc	2468 cc
Approximate power output	60 bhp	60 bhp	80 bhp
@ rpm	3500	3500	4000
Gearbox	3 speed non-synchro	4 speed non-synchro	4 speed non-synchro
Brakes	Mechanical: Early cars Perrot Later cars Cable	Cable	Cable
Drums	12″ diameter	14″ diameter	14″ diameter
Number built	501	228	5
Body Styles	2 door Salonette 4 door Saloon 4 seater Tourer 2 seater with dickey Speed model	2 door Salonette 4 door Saloon 4 seater Tourer 2 seater with dickey Speed model Coupe 4 door de luxe Saloon	4 seat Sports/Racing

Early versions of the Mark I were built with bolt-on wheels, and photographs show these clearly, even though retouched. Above & Below *pictures are actual production bodies, the two-door tourer* Centre *was not produced in numbers.*

The early two-door salonette displays most of the features of all saloon variants. Centre: *comfortable seats.* Below: *the 'boot' which offered plenty of space and a rexine cover for the luggage.*

MG S

These pictures show all the essential details of the early production Mark I chassis, engine and comprehensive instrumentation. The housing behind the bulkhead hid reserve oil and fuel tanks (one gallon each).

Above: *A very early prototype salonette Chassis No. E100, which started life as an eight-cylinder Morris.* Below: *the production form of the two-door salonette, both fabric and coachbuilt versions.*

The very handsome Mark I 4-door saloon.

Interior view of the well appointed saloon.

The Mark I open 4-door tourer with boot.

Hood up view of the same model: this is a 1930 model car with cable brakes.

The two-seater Mark I with hood up was not the best looking M.G.!

With hood down looks improved however, and the 'dickey' seat at the rear offered a useful emergency seat . . . . or possibly isolation for a chaperone?

In the early 1960's The M.G. Car Co. Ltd., rebuilt a Mark I Speed Model. Above: *Before* Below: *After rebuild. The saloon in the upper picture suffered many of the missing parts to the restored car.*
Opposite page: *This Mark I Speed Model* (*driver not known*) *completed the 1931 Monte Carlo Rally: an event in which M.G's have competed many times through the years*

HOTEL RENAISSANCE HOTEL
HOTEL
ALLYE AUTOMOBILE INTERNAT
ARRIVÉE
21 JANVIER 1931

Miss Amy Johnson, the aviatrix, was presented with a Mark I Salonette by Lord Nuffield in recognition of her achievements — it had a distinctive radiator mascot (Left).

Below: *The first Mark II: an unusual two-door two-light Salonette.*

The Mark II chassis was similar in layout to the Mark I, but heavier in execution. The four-speed gearbox had a remote control change speed lever — the first on an M.G. — which incorporated a Yale lock anti-thief device.

The two-seater Mark II was similar to the Mark I — in fact the same main body section was used with wider mudguards.

There were several tourer versions of the Mark II. These two pictures of a four-door open tourer display the well-proportioned lines. A similar version was available with a saloon-type boot and there was a Speed Model too, but these were built in very small numbers.

The 4-door Saloon de Luxe was offered for sale until 1933, but it sold slowly at £695.

The standard 4-door Saloon (Above), *and two-door Salonette* (Below) *were similar to the Mark I variants.*

A special Saloon de Luxe for Col. Grahame Deakin.
Side elevation of the same car.

Artist Gordon Crosby had this Saloon de Luxe in 1931.
Rear view of Gordon Crosby's car.

Three views of the two-seater Coupe version of Mark II — believed built by Carbodies.

The four-seater coupe Mark II version.

Above: *a one-off built for Harold Parkinson on Mark II chassis.*

Below: *another one-off which survives.*

A rather unhandsome 18/80 to prove that not all coachbuilders succeeded in making an attractive car! This one was built for a Mrs. Gough.

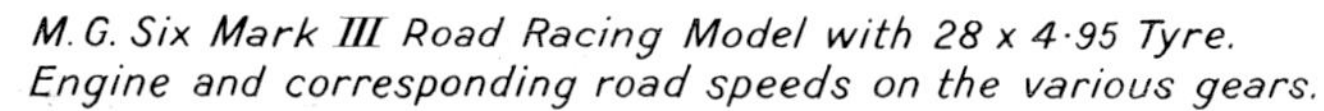

The Mark III power unit, showing the special SU carburettors and different dynamo/distributor/water pump layout.
Below: *The theoretical performance graph for the Mark III.*

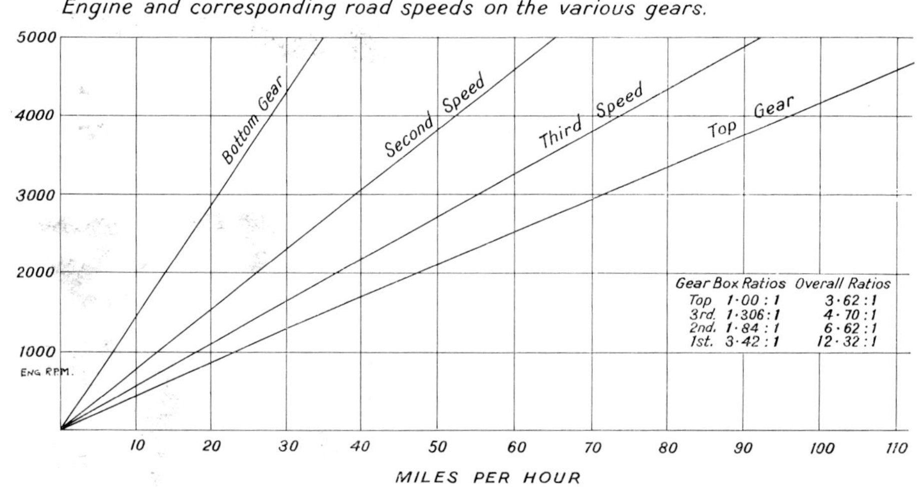

The 1930 Double-Twelve 18/100 Mark III, or "Tigress". The finish was cream with brown mudguards. The dual rear shock absorbers and extra fuel tanks can be seen on the right: total fuel capacity was 25 gallons.

Above & Centre: *The 1930 Olympia Show car.* Below: *The car sold to Lord Rothschild. Both of these cars are now owned by Christopher Barker.*

CHAPTER THREE

Early Midgets

What prompted Kimber to consider the 8 hp market as one with potential is not clear. Before the 1928 Motor Show all M.G.'s had been in the middle price range, with an accent on a well appointed touring car with adequate speed, rather than the attributes of a true sports car. The 18/80 was a logical step forward with this policy — the Midget, announced shortly after the Six, appeared to break new ground.

Of course, who could fail to notice the success of the Sports Austin Seven? The introduction of the Morris Minor in 1928 must have fired Kimber's imagination, for what Austin had done, surely M.G. could emulate or even improve upon?

Modifications to the Morris Minor to make the new Midget were very few: virtually fitting the neat two-seater body and its exterior fittings. Reasons for this were undoubtedly associated with the rush to get a car to Olympia, for modifications did follow, many of which improved on the original specification.

The engine was a four cylinder unit, with two bearing crankshaft. It had an overhead camshaft, driven through two sets of bevel gears and vertical shaft, the latter being formed in part by the dynamo armature. A flexible coupling was used to transfer the drive from the armature to a short shaft in the cylinder head. The front crank bearing was a double-row ball race, but all other bearings were white metal. The crankshaft was entered into the crankcase through the front end, which allowed the main bearings to be supported all round by the crankcase, giving great strength.

Porting was along the left-hand side of the cylinder head with inlets siamesed, as were exhaust ports for cylinders 2 and 3. Valves were slightly inclined in the head, and were operated by finger-type cam followers pivoting on eccentrically drilled bushes off two shafts, one either side of the head. This basic design featured in all the o.h.c. Midget, Magna and Magnette range, and proved a major factor in the success of these cars.

The clutch, chassis and axles of the M-type were all Morris parts, although the springs had decreased camber and the steering layout modified. The steering column was steeply raked, and the gear lever cranked down, giving a lower driving position.

The whole car was designed as a *sporty* rather than sports car, but provided such good roadholding and performance compared with its competitors that it was soon referred to as a "real sports car" by the press.

That it would be a success was fairly obvious from initial demands at the 1928 Motor Show, but it was six months before production commenced in earnest. The car was in considerable demand and sold well for the next three years.

Racing was indulged in by private owners at Club meetings during 1929, but it was the entry of a team of cars in the 1930 Double Twelve Race, and at Le Mans the same year which produced the first Midget racing car.

The Double Twelve Midget was modified but slightly from standard specification. The engine had improved valve timing, a larger carburettor and Brooklands exhaust system. A larger fuel tank was fitted and a host of detail modifications were carried out. The bodywork was slightly narrower than standard, and had cut away door sides but was otherwise along similar lines.

Extra performance was achieved only by increasing the usable rev. range of the engine, and having only 850 cc it was severely handicapped in the 1100 cc class, and was no match for the Rileys and Amilcars.

Winter efforts which culminated in an M.G. being the first 750 cc car to achieve 100 mph led to the racing man being offered a 750 cc vehicle of immense capability for 1931: the Montlhery Midget, or C-type.

The engine followed M-type practice almost exactly, but was capable of very high crankshaft speeds, thanks to a new valve timing, which incidentally was adopted for most subsequent o.h.c. models.

A four-speed gearbox of ENV manufacture allowed full use of the new found power to be made.

The success of the C-type can be almost wholly attributed to chassis design however. The frame was a ladder-type, and axles underslung — the rear one actually passing over the chassis. Axles followed M-type design, but the whole chassis gave a really low centre of gravity. Spring mounting was by a pivot at the leading end, the rear end sliding in trunnions. This eliminated the sideways winding effect experienced with shackled springs on corners. Wheels were of Rudge pattern for the first time on a Midget.

Throughout 1931 the C-type was unbeatable in its class, appearing in both supercharged and unsupercharged forms to take best advantage from handicaps applied in various events.

During 1932 more power was made available by use of a cross-flow cylinder head, which in turn necessitated the use of a counterbalanced crankshaft. Supercharging at up to 14 lbs p.s.i. boost became used, and towards the end of the year 12″ brake drums became available, and most cars used in racing were so equipped to assist retardation, which had become problematical from the high speeds now being achieved.

Coincident with the introduction of the C there came a D-type. This was a four-seater Midget, which was, in effect, a lengthened C-type chassis, but it was powered by an M-type power unit so that the resulting car was not a fast one. Sales were never very good, and those who bought them found that with four up there were problems in handling.

For 1933 a whole new range of Midgets was announced, and the Motor Show of 1932 was presented with a sensation similar to that of the introduction of the original Midget.

The J-series was a refinement of the C and D series into production form, of which the J2 is the best known, considered by many as typical of the M.G. sports car, and certainly it paved the road towards the modern sports car with low final drive ratio and a high revving power unit.

Chassis layout followed C-type patterns, and the engine was a productionised version of the 1932 C-type unit, with crossflow 8-port head and all. Twin S.U. carburettors were featured, and maximum power was quoted at 5500 rpm: with a two-bearing crankshaft!

Bodywork broke new grounds. It was very simple, and yet truly attractive. Square ended, swept up over the scuttle, cut away at the doors — it looked a real sports car. A huge fuel tank was mounted vertically at the rear, which ensured a good touring range. The cycle-type mudguards set the whole car off.

A four-seater version, the J1, was offered in open and closed form, very similar in layout to the D-type.

A supercharged J2 called the J3 was announced and, apart from a 750 cc unit which was similar to early C-types, was a J2 in every respect, though the performance was rather better if suitable sparking plugs could be found!

The racing version of the J-range was the J4. This also was basically a J2 although the steering track-rod was divided at the centre like the K-types. Brake gear featured the 12″ drums which were found on the Magna. The J4 was a really fast car, several Brooklands laps in excess of 100 mph being recorded, and the lap record for Class H at Ards is forever held by Hugh Hamilton in one of these cars at 77.20 mph, set in 1933. "Hammy" was one of the very few drivers to extract the full potential of this little car, which could be a real handful at speed.

The success of the Midget ensured the success of M.G., and there can be little doubt that the continuous development of the type from a brisk performer through the first Class H car to exceed 100 mph to a real 80 mph small sports car did much to capture the imagination of the public.

At the same time, the cars engendered much adverse criticism. This was propagated largely by those who had owned an oldish example in poor repair. Early J2's certainly did not live up to the 80 mph expectations, but as soon as fuel starvation problems were overcome there were few which were not capable of at least 75 mph on the level with screen down.

Keeping that class of performance was solely a matter of maintenance, and as with many more exotic machines, they were better left alone than meddled with by those who had not the knowledge!

The vertical dynamo also had its share of criticism: not so much for its own malfunction as because oil was reputed to run over the instrument draining from the vertical shaft above. Again this only was experienced by those who had removed the head, and not taken care to align the drive on reassembly.

Given careful maintenance these cars all gave, and indeed still give, good service. They certainly were capable of taking far more hard use than any comparable competitor at any price, witness of which fact is that so many have survived to the present time, in spite of maltreatment.

SPECIFICATIONS

	M	*C*	*D*	*J1*	*J2*	*J3*	*J4*
Bore and Stroke	57 x 83 mm	57 x 71 mm	57 x 83 mm	57 x 83 mm	57 x 83 mm	57 x 71 mm	57 x 71 mm
Capacity	847 cc	746 cc	847 cc	847 cc	847 cc	746 cc	746 cc
Valve operation	Single ohc	Single ohc	Single ohc	Single ohc	Single ohc	Single ohc	Single ohc
Approx. power output (un S/C)	20 (1929/30) 27 (1930/32)	36 (1931) 44 (1932)*	27	36	36	—	—
@ rpm	4500	6000	4500	5500	5500	—	—
Approx. power output S/C**	—	52 (1931)†	—	—	—	45	72
@ rpm	—	6500	—	—	—	6000	6000
Gearbox	3 speed Non synchro	4 speed Non synchro	3 speed Non synchro	4 speed Non synchro	4 speed Non synchro	4 speed Non synchro	4 speed Non synchro
Brakes	Mechanical, operated by Bowden cables, from single cross shaft.						
Drums (Diameter)	8″	8″	8″	8″	8″	8″	12″
Number built	3235	44	250	380	2083	22	9
Body Types	2 seater sports Sportsmans' Coupe	2 seat sports/racing	4 seat tourer Salonette	4 seat tourer Salonette	2 seat sports	2 seat sports	2 seat sports/racing

* with cross flow head

† with 'AA' head

** Supercharged power outputs vary with boost pressure and fuel. Figures given are taken from M.G. Factory graphs.

All power outputs are quoted at advised maximum "safe" sustained engine speeds.

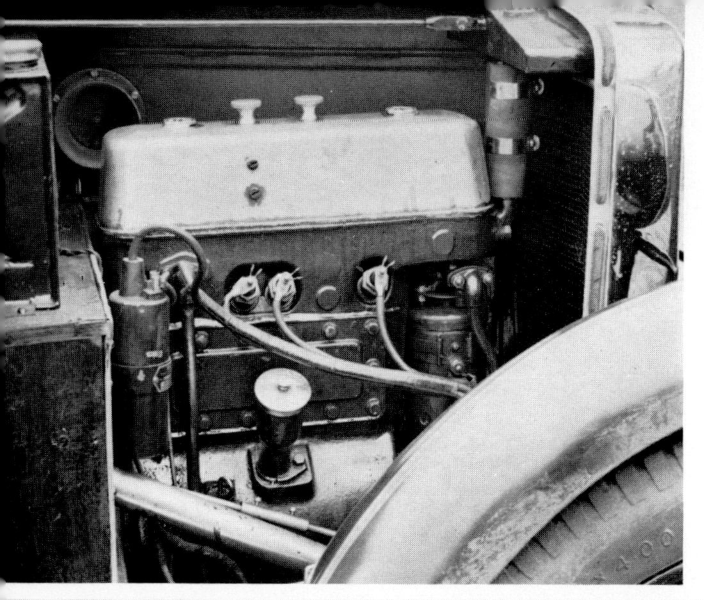

The offside view of an M-type engine. The front oil drain pipe was altered on later engines. Note the fuel tank behind the engine.

Above: *The early M-type chassis with transmission handbrake, and rod-operated wheel brakes. Its Morris Minor heredity can easily be seen.*

Nearside of the engine. This car was an early Oxford-built one — see guarantee plate.

Various views of early M-types. WL 7171 was a demonstrator car used in contemporary road tests. RX 5971 was used by H. S. Linfield of the 'Light Car' in the 1930 Classic Trials.

The car which made 100 consecutive ascents of Beggars Roost without stopping the engine.

The Double Twelve M-type. It was finished with brown body and cream wings, and priced at £245 — £60 more than the standard car.

The late 1932-model metal-panelled body.

The Sportsman's Coupe was a handsome little car — both fabric (Above) *and metal-panelled* (Centre and Below) *bodies are shown.*

The interior of the Coupe, showing the excellent and comfortable appointments.

The prototype Coupe and (Centre) *early production variants all of which are different!*

An early University Motors special body — the "University Foursome". Perhaps it should have been a two-plus-two-very-small-halfsome?

One of the most attractive special bodies — the Jarvis M-type. Priced at £255 it must have been an attractive buy for those wanting something different.

The Montlhery Midget or C-type, swept the board in 750cc Class Racing in 1931.

RX 8306 is here supercharged, and was subsequently owned by the Evans brothers, although this was not their famous sprint car.

More shots of the C-type displaying its attractive shape from all angles. The radiator cowl was discarded after the 1931 Double Twelve in which the cars filled the first 5 places.

The D-type was essentially a lengthened C-type chassis, fitted with four seater-bodywork and powered by an M-type engine.

Above: *a prototype, and* (Below) *the production version displaying the attractive line of the body: which made up for the lack of performance.*

The J-type engine as fitted to the J1 and J2.

The J-chassis shows the weight to be low and forward.

The J3 engine was the same as a J2 externally and only differed internally in the length of its stroke.

Above and Left: *The J1 was the logical progression from the D-type and in tourer form had far better performance.*

Left and Below: *The J1 salonette shared the same coachwork with the F1 Magna, but the shorter bonnet made it less attractive.*

The archtypal Midget: The J2. The 1932 version is considered by many to be one of the classic sports cars of all time, though the hood does not enhance appearances.

The J3 looked very similar to the J2. JB 1047 was the car which took the 24 hour Class H record in 1933.

Below: *The racing J4 was immediately identifiable with its less exotic brothers. Only nine of these were built however.*

The 1933/4 J2 was the first Midget to be fitted with swept wings, and opinions are divided as to the effect of this on its looks.

Like most other models, the J2 suffered at the hands of the specialist coachbuilders — the results in these cases are less attractive than the works bodies. Above: *A Czechoslovakian offering by Uhlik, and* (Below) *one from Van den Plas.*

CHAPTER FOUR

Magnas and Magnettes

With the success of the 8 hp Midget, and the wide price disparity with the 18/80 range, it must have been obvious that a car was necessary which would fill the gap left with the cessation of production of the old side-valve cars.

The Wolseley Hornet was introduced early in 1930, and it was possessed of a nice little engine. The rest of the car was pretty uninspired especially as a basis for a sports car, being merely a lengthened Morris Minor: it even had the Minor body!

Kimber must have considered the possibility of a 12 hp Midget, but fortunately was not tempted to put it to trial, probably having tried a Hornet! Also, of course, plans were rushing ahead with the Double-Twelve Midget and with a more important car which paved the way for the C-type Montlhery Midget. These would have kept the Design team more than slightly busy.

Thus it was September 1931 before the first 12 hp M.G. Magna was announced: a "light six", which was M.G.'s offering to the motoring public's latest fad in the search for smooth running engines.

The chassis followed very closely the layout of the C and D-type Midgets, sharing axles, steering gear and brakes. Like the D, the F-type had a rivetted chassis frame, with underslung rear axle. The wheelbase was 8″ longer than the D, to help accommodate the extra engine length. The gearbox was an ENV unit similar to that fitted to the racing C-type.

The engine was closely similar to the Hornet unit, and has been called an "M-type plus 2 cylinders". The latter comment is an over-simplification, however. True it was a six cylinder unit, and true it bore more than a passing resemblance to the M unit.

Both crankshaft and camshaft ran in four bearings, the front being a ball race as in the Midget, the intermediate bearings being formed of aluminium housings containing white-metal lined bronze bushes — like the old Morris Oxford units. These housings were clamped around the crankshaft and then the whole crank was fed through the front of the crankcase. The inter bearings were clamped with long through bolts. Big ends were of white metal applied direct to the rods, although some early engines had aluminium rods, which necessitated the use of white metalled bronze bushes.

Camshaft drive was by a vertical shaft of obvious M-type origins, and the valve gear and porting was closely similar, the valve timing being of the earlier M-type variety. The whole engine was clad in sheet metal, presumably to disguise it from its Wolseley forebear!

Drive was taken through a clutch of larger proportions than the M-type to the ENV gearbox already mentioned.

Body styles originally offered were four-seat tourer and a close coupled salonette. Both models were attractive, and generally handled well, if somewhat lacking in power at the top end of the scale.

The engine was undeniably smooth, in spite of being mounted rigidly in the chassis, and was able to provide a continuous flow of torque from tick-over speeds right up to maximum. The gearbox had ideal ratios, and the combination provided was truly delightful.

Towards the time of the 1932 Motor Show, the specification of the car was changed slightly, 12″ brake drums being the major improvement. A two-seater, using J2 pattern body was offered and called the F2, while the four-seater became known as the F3.

At that same Motor Show however was introduced a far more important range of vehicles. Powered by an 1100 cc six-cylinder unit, it was dubbed the "Magnette", or K-series.

The chassis again followed the now established layout of M.G.'s although it was both longer and wider, and had more track. The steering gear was given a patented divided track-rod layout, which was assumed to give less kickback at the steering wheel: the drag link being attached to an idler arm to the left of centre of the axle beam. Two short track rods were also attached to this idler. The layout appears to have been at least partly successful if a little expensive.

Brake gear followed M.G. practice, although electron brake drums of 13″ diameter were used, which had steel liners shrunk in.

The engine was a much improved version of the Magna unit, having crossflow head, and a much stronger crankshaft and camshaft. The cam followers were modified to take some of the loading off the cams. Porting was six to a side, and of positively enormous size.

No less than 3 S.U. carburettors were fitted, and ignition was supplied by a B.T.H. Magneto mounted alongside the offside of the cylinder block. A low overlap valve-timing was used, which allowed a very low engine tick-over, which in turn eliminated "creep" when stationary, due to peculiarities of the transmission.

No clutch was used, drive being taken direct to a Wilson-type pre-selector gearbox manufactured by E.N.V. The selector quadrant being mounted in the position occupied by the gear lever of a conventional gearbox. For those unfamiliar with this type of gearbox it should be explained that there are no gears to shift as such. There is a continuous gear train, made of 4 clusters of gears: providing reverse, 1st, 2nd and 3rd gears. A cone clutch provided direct top gear. Brake bands contracted to stop one or other of the gear clusters revolving, which altered the gear ratio from engine to rear axle.

The operation of the gearbox was in two stages: firstly selection of the gear required, with the hand operated lever, and engagement which was provided by operating the foot pedal located where one might normally find the clutch pedal. This enabled pre-selection of a gear and immediate engagement without the need for synchronisation of hand and foot movements, and indeed without much effort from the brain!

The pre-selector was originally designed as an alternative to the synchromesh system, which was still far from perfected. It was however expensive to make, and complicated to work upon, which resulted in much unwarranted criticism of the type.

It was cost and the onset of efficient automatic gearboxes which finally killed it however, but for many years, even as recently as 1957, pre-selector gearboxes were fitted to racing cars.

The coachwork offered with the Magnette was as remarkable as its mechanical specification. A full four-seater saloon, of pillarless construction, which offered 70 mph plus (at 5,000 rpm!) and good appointments at a price only slightly higher than the Riley Nine: but with a six cylinder engine and far better handling and acceleration.

Early in 1933, an open four-seater was finally announced and a two-seater shorter wheelbase car called a K2, the four-seater and saloon being called K1's. The mechanical specification of the open cars featured a two-plate clutch, and manual four-speed gearbox, and standard M.G. valve timing.

The engine of the saloon was known as the KA, while that of the open cars was the KB.

The odd sized porting of the Magnette has already been mentioned, and this led to a somewhat disappointing power output. The KA, with its "slow" valve timing could only manage an output of 5% better than the Magna unit. The KB improved by a further 7%, thanks to its timing, but this was achieved at the expense of using 5,500 rpm.

The K-types could be made to perform well, but only by really using the gearbox freely, and thus the cars did not gain the acclaim they should have received.

One K-type which did perform well however was the K3 racing Magnette. Probably the best known M.G. model, it is certainly one of the most successful 1100 cc racing cars ever built.

The K3 was basically a supercharged K2. Engine was almost standard KB specification, although special valves and valve springs were used, and the bearings had high duty metal applied. A supercharger was mounted ahead of the radiator, and the high boost employed ensured adequate filling of the large porting already referred to. Power output was raised by a factor of nearly three over its unblown brother.

The chassis was similar to the K2, although a cross-brace was fitted as in the K1 behind the gearbox, which was a pre-selector. Special brake drums in which the liners were screwed in were used, following trouble in the car's first outings.

For a new model to win class awards at major events on its first outing became something of an M.G. achievement from 1930, and the K3 won both its class award and team award in the Mille Miglia of 1933. This was followed with countless victories.

During 1933 the Magna range was up-dated with the L-type range, in which a version of the 1100 cc K-type engine was used to improve the possibilities for improving performance of the range, and also as a step towards standardisation.

The engine, known as the KC, was in fact a KB unit with coil ignition and twin carburettors. The KB clutch and gearbox were featured, the latter, incidentally being essentially the same as that fitted to the J-Midgets.

The L-Magna in four-seat and saloon (L1) and two-seater (L2) forms was a pretty car, although Kimber made one of his rare *gaffes* in coachbuilding design with an unattractive continental Coupe.

Later in 1933 the K1 and K2 ranges were provided with more power, derived by enlarging the engine to 1271 cc by increasing the stroke. Twin carburettors and coil ignition were fitted to this unit, which also featured a clutch, in spite of the use of the pre-selector gearbox.

This clutch was operated by the pedal and its purpose was to disconnect the gearbox from the engine when neutral was "engaged". This allowed the use of the "faster" valve timing, since pre-selector creep was now abolished. Oddly enough this simple and elegant solution to the problem was not used by any other manufacturer, who seemed to prefer the additional complications of automatic clutches or fluid couplings.

The new power unit was dubbed the KD, and gave the K1 a new lease of life, with 25% more power than when originally introduced.

While most manufacturers were content to introduce new models each year, M.G. seemed to do so every six months, for in March 1934 a brand new range of Magnettes was announced — the N-type.

The N was important because chassis design was changed, and because it was to be the final small six M.G., as well as the last of the single o.h.c. cars to remain in production.

The engine was a developed form of the KD unit. Confusion exists as to the piston displacement, but in spite of factory records, personal experience has led the writer to the conclusion that cubic capacity was the same as for the KD. Modifications were fairly far reaching, involving cylinder block, cylinder head, inlet manifold, lubrication system and clutch. The modifications produced a power output increase of a further 25%, which endowed the N-type with a good turn of speed.

The gearbox was similar to the L-type, although ratios at first were of the "trials" type, with two low starting gears and two much higher ratios.

The chassis deserves special mention, since it was the first M.G. since 1930 not to have a simple ladder frame, the side members being wider at the rear than the front. Also outrigger members at each side and the rear carried the body, these being insulated by Silentbloc bushes from the main frame.

Bodywork was open two- or four-seater type, in which the "slab-tank" was no longer worn, the fuel tank being covered by a shapely tail. Shortly after announcement of the N-type two additional body styles were announced, the Allingham 2/4-seater which resurrected the dickey seat, and an Airline Coupe. Few of either type were actually produced, probably 12 of each, and it is odd that nowhere in the Press can one find reference to the 'ND' of which 40 or so were built. This model was certainly built and apparently used the unsold K2 bodies. It proved popular with the trials fraternity.

For 1935 the mechanical specification was altered slightly, reverting to close ratio gears and the bodywork was revised with a lower scuttle and front hinged doors. A slatted radiator grille like the 18/80's and contemporary PB was used, and this version was known in the Factory as the NB.

Reverting to 1934, a racing version of the N, the NE, was especially developed for the T.T. in which superchargers were banned for the first year. With all the odds against it, an NE won the race, on handicap, being faster than all other finishers but two 4½-litre engined vehicles.

Also in 1934 the KN saloon was announced, which offered the K pillarless saloon fitted with N-type power unit and gearbox, which at least endowed the car with sporting acceleration. An open four-seater version of the KN was sold by University Motors of London as the "U.M. Speed Model Magnette", quite a few of which appear to have survived.

However, by 1935 the age of the 'small six' was coming to a close — rubber mounted large displacement 'fours' providing better torque characteristics. The NB carried on in production into 1936, its high revving and exceptionally smooth engine competing successfullt with less sophisticated units.

The Magnas and Magnettes were mostly good cars, the F being underrated, the L-type rather too narrow for its performance, and the K1 and K2 rather heavy. The N's were probably the best of the o.h.c. M.G.'s having adequate performance in standard form and yet being capable of taking much more without upsetting its good manners.

SPECIFICATIONS

	F1	*F2*	*F3*	*L1*	*L2*	*K1(KA)*	*K1(KB)*	*K1(KD)*	*K2(KB)*	*K2(KD)*	*K3*	*NA/NB/ ND/KN*	*NE*
Bore & Stroke	57 x 83 mm	57 x 83 mm	57 x 83 mm	57 x 71 mm	57 x 71 mm	57 x 71 mm	57 x 71 mm	57 x 83 mm	57 x 71 mm	57 x 83 mm	57 x 71 mm	57 x 83 mm	57 x 83 mm
Capacity	1271 cc	1271 cc	1271 cc	1086 cc	1086 cc	1086 cc	1086 cc	1271 cc	1086 cc	1271 cc	1086 cc	1271 cc	1271 cc
Valve operation	All models: single overhead camshaft.												
Approx. Power Output	37	37	37	41	41	39	41	48.5	41	48.5	120	56	70
@ r.p.m.	4100	4100	4100	5500	5500	5500	5500	5500	5500	5500	6500	5500	6500
Gearbox	4 speed Non synchro	4 speed Non synchro	4 speed Non synchro	4 speed Non synchro	4 speed Non synchro	4 speed Pre-selector	4 speed Non synchro	4 speed Pre-selector	4 speed Non synchro	4 speed Pre-selector	4 speed Pre-selector	4 speed Non synchro	4 speed Non synchro
Brakes	All models: mechanical operated by Bowden cables from single central cross shaft.												
Drums (Diameter)	8″	12″	12″	12″	12″	13″	13″	13″	13″	13″	13″	12″ 13″(KN)	12″
Number built	114	40	94	486	90	54	74	53	16	4	33	NA/NB690 ND48 KN193	7
Body Types	4 seat open 4 seat Salonette	2 seat open	4 seat open 4 seat Salonette	4 seat open 4 seat saloon 2 seat coupe	2 seat open	4 seat saloon	4 seat tourer	4 seat saloon 4 seat open	2 seat open	2 seat open	2 seat racing	NA/NB: 2 seat open 4 seat open 2 seat coupe NA only: 2/4 seat open coupe ND: 2 seat open KN: 4 seat saloon	2 seat racing

The F-type Magna chassis followed closely the layout of the C & D types. The engine was a modified Wolseley Hornet unit.

Below: *The L-type Magna was very similar, but had the much improved 1100 cc engine and Wolseley gearbox, which was not quite so good.*

The F2 was introduced in 1932 — as can be seen the bodywork was closely similar to the J2, but it sported 12" brake drums.

The F1 four-seater made up for lack in performance with a rakish and fast look — and was one of the few pre-war M.G.'s with a nice looking hood.

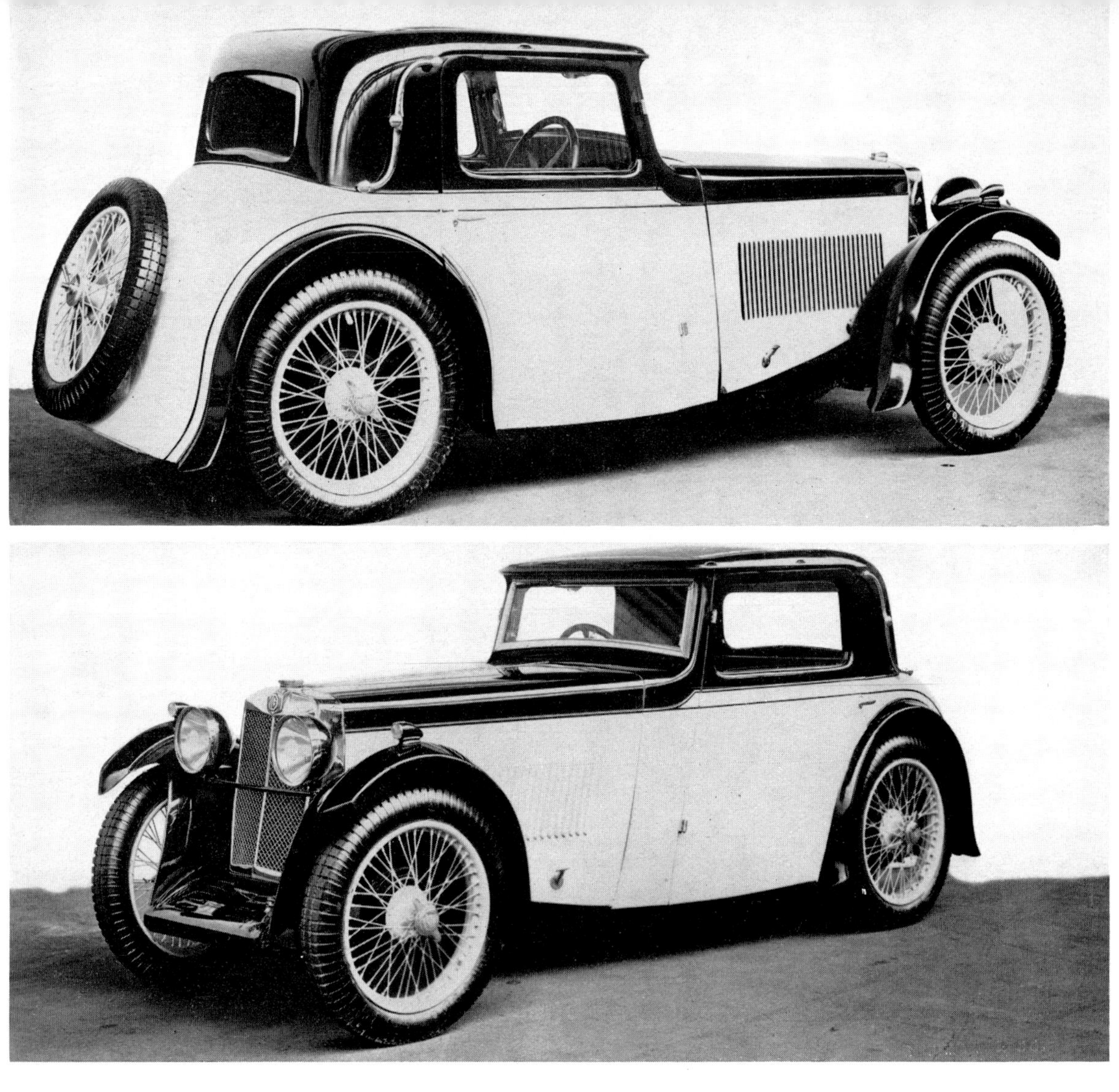

A rather stunted looking special bodied F1 by Abbey.

Below: *A more successful one by Stiles: several of these survive.*

The F1 salonette was a very low car. The upper photograph is of an early prototype, those below are differing production versions. The author owned one of these for two years and found it an enjoyable vehicle.

The L2 Magna is one of the more sought after pre-war M.G.'s now. It was very attractive, and even today a quick car, although roadholding is not up to the Magnette and Midget standards.

The L1 4-seater shared with the L2 a handsome line. JB 1270 is a prototype, with F-type scuttle. JB 1646 was a factory demonstrator.

Kimbers' folly! The L1 Continental Coupe, of which a hundred were built, and took as many weeks to sell!

It was, however, well appointed, offering its two occupants comfort, and plenty of room for baggage.

The four-seater L1 salonette was somewhat more practical, if a little top heavy.

The University Motors Folding-hood Foursome on an L-chassis — were any actually built, I wonder?

The original Magnette was a K1 Pillarless Saloon. JP 550 actually had chassis number K0251, and survives. The author considers this one of the most handsome closed M.G.'s of all time. It was, however, somewhat overweight for its 1100cc engine: later KD versions were better. Its super-equipped body harked back to 18/80 days.

Above: *Cecil Kimber in his special bodied K1 which was supercharged.*
Right: *Abbey-bodied K1, probably a 1934 model.*

Right: *Magnette bodied by Whittingham & Mitchel — this is on a KN chassis.*
Below: *Another Abbey bodied K1: this with a special steel boot and folding hood.*

The K1 tourer: all these being the earlier KB-engined version.

The K2 two-seater shared much of its chassis and running gear with the K3, but is actually a much rarer car.

The 1933 K3 — these are two of the Mille Miglia team cars, JB 1474 was driven by Rubin and Birkin, and is now in Australia, while JB 1475 was driven by Lurani and Eyston. This remains in the U.K.

K3 — the quintessence of the K Magnette theme. The chassis was rigged and well equipped — designed for 1,000 miles of rough roads. This is a 1934 version, with Marshall supercharger.

Jensen built this body for W. E. C. Watkinson on a K3 chassis. The original chassis has now emigrated to the U.S.A., but the body remains in the U.K. on a K2 chassis. It is all aluminium and very attractive.

The 1934 K3 Magnette (Above) *in prototype form, and* (Below) *in rebuilt form — this is the car which originally wore the coachwork shown opposite.*

The KN, (naturally dubbed "hot stuff" by the press!) was the final flowering of the K-type theme. The N-engine supplied the power it needed, and it proved more popular than earlier versions.

The N-type Magnette chassis (Above) *displays its salient features. The KN chassis* (Below) *differed in respect of the length and shape of the frame. Both models shared the 1271cc engine* (Right).

The NA two-seater was somewhat tall amidships, but the duotone colour scheme did much to alleviate the height.

The later NB version had a lower scuttle line, which allowed a reversal of the colour scheme. The rear seat passengers in the four seater (Above) *tended to act as the pendulum bob however!*

Another Whittingham and Mitchel offering: the so-called Allingham 2-4 seater. A small folding seat could be opened in the tail, which unlike earlier dickeys was enclosed by the hood. The car above was driven by W. E. C. Watkinson on the 1934 RAC Rally.

The Abbey-bodied two-seater looked even taller than its standard production brother! A factory built ND looked very similar to this, and was produced in larger numbers.

The Cresta bodied NA, said to have been designed and built by Bertelli.

Another Abbey-bodied car, a Coupe this time. Still a little heavy towards the rear.

A continental N type, built by Sportcar A.G. of Zurich.

CHAPTER FIVE

The Midget Grows Up

The Early Midgets of chapter three included the introduction of the J series. By the end of 1933 though, the two bearing crankshaft was definitely feeling the strain, particularly in racing. A redesign of the power unit was called for.

If the F Magna had an engine which was an "M plus two", then that for the P was an "N minus two". In effect, cylinders 4 and 5 were removed from the block, leaving a four pot of comparatively large outside dimensions. The centre main bearing was steel of similar pattern to the N. The crankshaft was immensely robust compared with the J, although it was still not counterbalanced.

Cylinder head and camshaft design was very similar to the N, in fact the whole engine contained a maximum of parts interchangeable between Midget and Magnette. The clutch and gearbox were of similar pattern to the N.

The chassis followed J practice, although the larger brake drums of the L & N were used for the first time on a sports Midget. Open two or four seaters similar in general layout to the J, but much improved in detail, were offered, and a smart fastback coupe called an "Airline" became available shortly after introduction.

Unfortunately the PA as it subsequently became known, was suffering from a surfeit of weight, and full potential of this little car only becoming realised when supercharged. Supercharger kits were offered by several manufacturers, and M.G. took the unprecedented step of offering to continue the guarantee of the car provided one of the recommended units working at a maximum boost of five pounds per square inch was used.

Fierce competition, particularly from the Singer Nine Sports was being experienced however, and it had to be admitted that the 970 cc of this car were more than a match for the 850 of the M.G. — although the former car had a two bearing crankshaft. In 1935 therefore the cylinder bore was increased to 60mm, and together with other detail modifications the car became known as the PB. The later version is easily recognisable with its slatted radiator grille. The PB was a far superior car to its smaller brother in terms of performance, so that quite a few PA's were subsequently converted to PB specification to help sell them.

With supercharger fitted the PB had few equals in its day, and soon proved omnipotent in trials — a factory supported team known as the "Cream Crackers" being particularly successful. Even now many M.G. enthusiasts rate a blown PB as a good road car, although its roadholding is of a distinctly vintage character.

The racing customer for 1934 was offered the Q-type. This car had the same bore and stroke as other 750cc cars, and used the P-type block and head. A special crank and rods were used, the latter being increased in strength during the year and subsequently fitted to most racing o.h.c. models. A high pressure Zoller blower increased manifold pressures to around 2½ atmospheres, and the resulting power output almost matched that of the K3!

As in the K3 a pre-selector gearbox was used, but a non-operating clutch helped to cushion the loads on the rear axle. Wider track was obtained by using N-type axles, otherwise chassis and body design was more closely allied to the K3 than the P-type.

This little car was too fast for most drivers, its hard suspension causing it to leap from bump to bump around Brooklands. It had qualified success in short events, particularly in the hands of Bill Everitt, and a highly modified Q-type driven by George Harvey-Noble in 1937 holds the Brooklands Outer Circuit Class H record for all time at a phenomenal speed of 122.4 m.p.h.

However during 1934 H. N. Charles was investigating independent suspensions, and for 1935 M.G. offered a car which can only be called revolutionary: the R-type.

The power unit and gearbox were basically Q-type, but with improved induction system which hardly affected the power output, but reduced the appetite for sparking plugs.

Too much has already been written about its backbone frame and wishbone suspension, and reference to the photographs will tell the rest. The R-type's weaknesses were in its equal length rear wishbones and its rather too soft rear torsion bars, which made the car unstable under braking stresses. This was a small fault however, which could have been rectified. Indeed work had started with modification to the rear suspension, but this was not to be, for a halt was called to racing activities.

The R-type was nevertheless fairly successful, and could undoubtedly have been made more so, but racing costs money, and that was a commodity of which the small Berkshire factory was short, and one which the parent Nuffield Organisation was definitely *not* going to supply for such frivolous activities.

In 1936, rather than an improved P-type, the Midget was given a brand-new specification, so commenced the celebrated T-series Midgets: this one now being termed the TA.

The engine was derived from the recently introduced Morris Ten, just as that of the original Midget was derived from the contemporary Morris Minor. That it had push-rods and all its ports on one side of the head was taken as a sign of retrogression. It was also rubber mounted, so that the chassis frame was boxed at the forward end to retain stiffness.

The clutch and gearbox were also from the Morris Ten, but the rest of the car followed traditional M.G. layout although the bodywork was as spacious as the Magnette. Hydraulic brakes were used following the pattern set by the larger Morris based SA, recently introduced.

It has proved to be a good sound car, but was spoilt by an engine which did not respond to tuning and was not renowned for being robust in standard tune, it has thus obtained an undeserved reputation for being a bad car.

It was a very pleasant car to drive. Its large 4 cylinder unit had a most impressive low speed torque which endeared it to the trials brigade. Even the "Cream Crackers" and "Three Musketeers" teams eventually used T-types, although in a more modified form than the PB's used previously.

For 1939 a new engine was designed for the Morris Ten, and this formed the basis for the famous XPAG unit, which was to feature so prominently in M.G. fortunes for the next fifteen years.

A four cylinder pushrod o.h.v. unit, it bore little but superficial resemblance to the one it replaced. A new block, head and counterbalanced crankshaft were employed. Shell bearings were used in the connecting rods and main bearings.

All that the TA engine lacked, the new TB unit had. It was sound, had good combustion chamber and valve port design, was able to run at high speed and capable of being extensively tuned. When fitted to the T chassis the TB was born, but the car only had a very short life thanks to the workings of a criminal lunatic who plunged the world into a major war.

SPECIFICATIONS

	PA	*PB*	*QA*	*RA*	*TA*	*TB*
Bore x Stroke	57 x 83 mm	60 x 83 mm	57 x 71 mm	57 x 71 mm	63.5 x 102 mm	66.5 x 90 mm
Capacity	847 cc	939 cc	746 cc	746 cc	1292 cc	1250 cc
Valve operation	Single overhead camshaft				Pushrod o.h.v.	
Approx. power output	36 bhp	43 bhp	113 bhp	113 bhp	50 bhp	54 bhp
@ r.p.m.	5500	5500	7200	7200	4500	5200
Gearbox	4 speed non-synchro		4 speed pre-selector		4 speed synchro on 3 & 4	4 speed synchro 2, 3 & 4
Brakes	Mechanical, operated by cables				Lockheed hydraulic	
Drums (diam.)	12″	12″	12″	12″	9″	9″
Number built	1973*	526	8	10	3003	379

*27 PA chassis were converted to PB and given PB chassis numbers, these have been deducted from the total.

The P-type Midget was a more rugged car than the J, owing much to experience gained with the Magna and Magnettes.

The PA two-seater was a smart little car — looking more natural than the later J2 in swept wings. Normal colour scheme was two-tone red, green or blue as can be discerned below.

The PB was the M.G. answer to the threat from Singer — a larger engine. This transformed the Midget and now it really was the best small sports car of 1935/36.
On the next page: *A PB in typically English surroundings.*

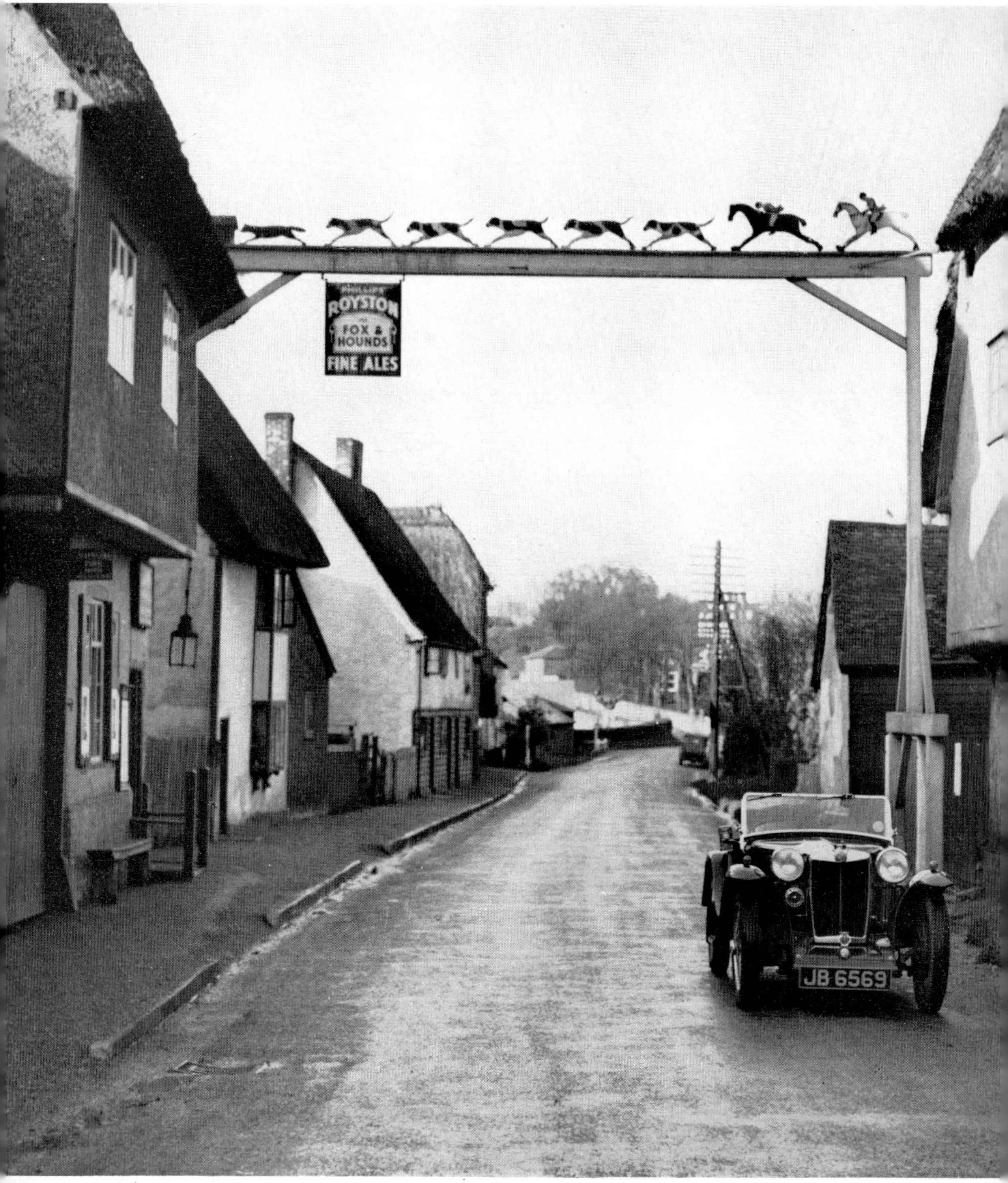
ROYSTON
FOX &
HOUNDS
FINE ALES
JB 6569

The PA four-seater had the grace of the Magna four-seater, but like the N version the rear seat passengers were rather too far back for stability.

The first G.T. fastback? The Airline Coupe was a truly attractive little car. Some were panelled in aluminium which must have helped performance.

A brace of special bodied P-types. Above: *by Hanni of Zurich and* (Below) *by Abbey. Neither is as attractive as the standard car.*

The original Q-car! The Q-type Midget had around 110 bhp on tap from its 750cc.

The cockpit was uncompromisingly for competition use.

But it looked right — the only problem was it was too fast for its chassis.

The R-type was the last H. N. Charles designed M.G. It was revolutionary. These two pictures were taken since the second World War, but no R-type has run in anger since 1955. The chassis (Opposite) *was rugged but well thought out.*

The R-type body was pretty too.

The TA, introduced in 1936, was largely Nuffield inspired. The chassis, however, shows close similarity with the P-type even though larger in execution.

The TA was well proportioned, profiting from larger dimensions than its predecessors. The TB looked identical, until the bonnet was opened.

Everything was laid out in traditional M.G. style, and it was not long before the T-Series was accepted as a "real" M.G.

The Tickford Coupe, built by Salmons of Newport Pagnell, which factory was later used for the production of Aston Martin cars, was a delightful little car.

The hood could be run folded (Above) *or in Coupe de Ville style* (Left).

This one is believed to be the prototype for the Tickford.

The tail treatment is more attractive, but probably more expensive.

The very rare Airline Coupe T-type.

Below: *A one-off factory built T Midget here being collected by its owner from the Managing Director.*

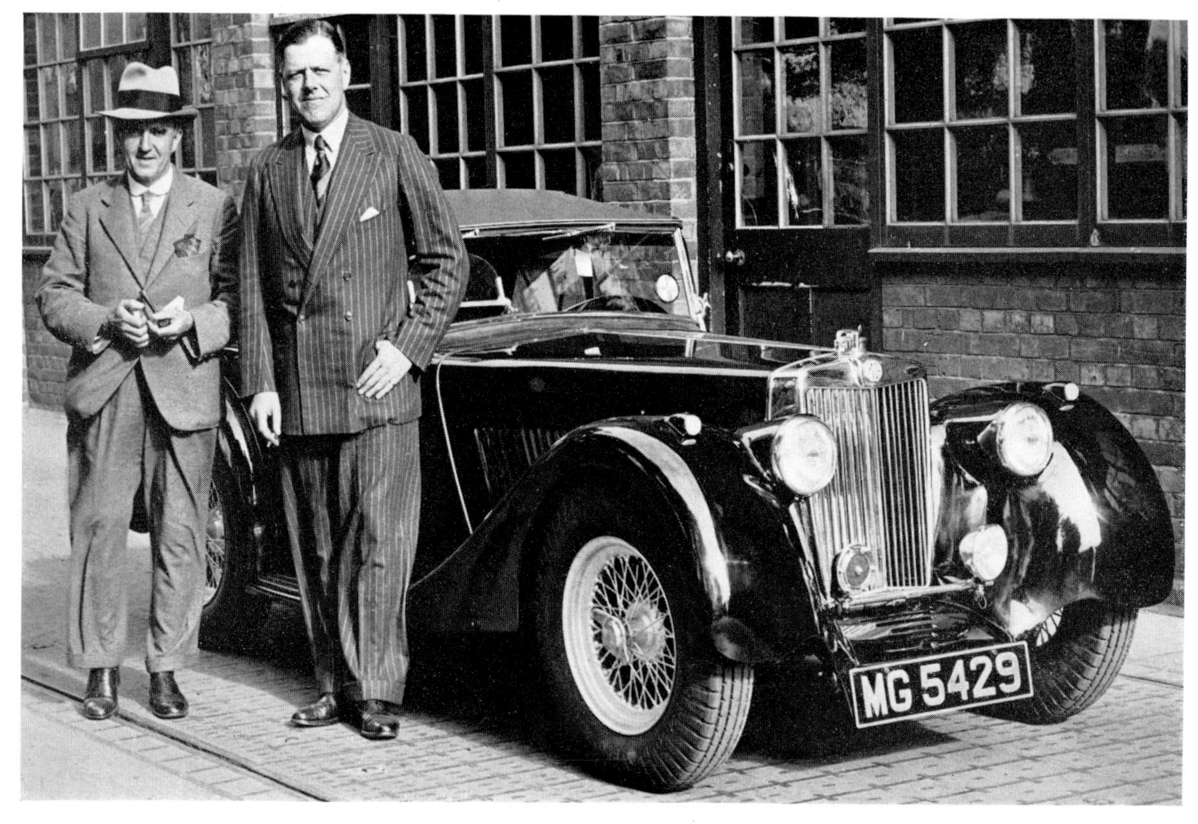

CHAPTER SIX

Pre-war Comfort

More dissention exists in M.G. circles when discussing the S-V-W range than any other pre-war group of cars, and is rivalled only by that surrounding the later post war Magnettes.

Had it not been for the policy change in 1935, the SA might well have been a Magnette racing car based on the R-type, and the T-type was already taking the form of an independently sprung large saloon car powered by a Blackburne built V8 engine known around the factory as "Queen Mary". But this was not to be, which was probably just as well since we might not still have had M.G.'s to argue about.

The SA which was introduced late in 1935 replaced the KN Magnette. It was in fact cheaper, but offered considerably more in terms of comfort and the manner in which performance was delivered.

The chassis, based on the Wolseley 18, might be referred to as an up-dated version of the old 18/80. A 2.2 litre six cylinder engine, with pushrod operated valves supplied the power, and a crash gearbox transferred this from a clutch (shades of 18/80 again) to the conventional rear axle. Front axle owed something to M.G. racing practice, having torque reaction cables, but brakes were hydraulically operated on the Lockheed system.

Coachwork was quite breathtaking. The saloon announced first had smooth low lines, and plenty of space, all within the wheelbase. Performance was adequate, and achieved in relative silence.

The whole car appeared to offer all that the recently announced 3½ litre Bentley did at less than one-quarter the cost. In fact it did represent good value for money, and proved reasonably successful, bringing M.G. ownership to a much wider public.

A four-seater tourer by Charlesworth and a really handsome Tickford Coupe by Salmons followed a year after first announcement, increasing the appeal of the car.

Over its three years currency the car was progressively improved, with larger engine, synchromesh gearbox and a host of detail changes which now make historians wince somewhat!

In 1936 with the Midget replaced by the T-series, a new Magnette was awaited with interest. The 1½ litre, VA series, was something of a disappointment.

The car was a scaled down SA, with four cylinder power unit of similar bore and stroke giving rather more than 1½ litres displacement. Power output was actually lower than that of the NA, and since the car was heavy, acceleration was not up to the expected levels.

In point of fact the overall performance was quite reasonable and the car was better appointed than the old Magnette range. It appealed, like the 2 litre, to a new type of customer and sold well, but by no stretch of the imagination was either car of the "sports" type.

By late 1938 both the SA and VA had been modified to overcome their many problems, but no new model had been released by M.G. for two years. By modern standards this may not seem abnormal, but when one reflects that the whole range of o.h.c. cars, some eleven distinct model types were produced in seven short years the results of the changes of Company Policy may be seen. However a new model was adjudged necessary.

At the 1938 Motor Show therefore the newly announced 2.6 litre M.G. was greeted with great interest and enthusiasm.

It was a considerably refined 2 litre, with much improved engine, gearbox and running gear. Coachwork followed a similar pattern to that of the earlier car. Like the TB Midget, the WA was killed by the Second World War.

SPECIFICATIONS

	SA	VA	WA
Bore & Stroke	69 × 102 mm (1936/7) 69.5 × 102 mm (1937-9)	69.5 × 102 mm	73 × 10 2mm
Capacity	2288 cc (1936/7) 2322 cc (1937-9)	1549 cc	2561 cc
Valve operation		Pushrod overhead valves	
Approx. power output	78.5	55	95.5
@ rpm	4,200	4,400	4,400
Gearbox	4 speed non-synchro (1936/7) Synchro on 3 & 4 (1937-9)	4 speed Synchro on 2, 3 & 4	4 speed Synchro on 2, 3 & 4
Brakes		Lockheed hydraulic, mechanical handbrake	
Drums (diameter)	12″	10″	14″
Number built	2,738	2,407	369
Body Types	4 door saloon 4 seat Tourer Tickford Coupe	4 door saloon 4 seat Tourer Tickford Coupe	4 door saloon 4 seat Tourer Tickford Coupe

The chassis of the 2-litre SA was well laid out and in the pre-1930 M.G. tradition. The engine was accessible for service and featured down draught carburettors.

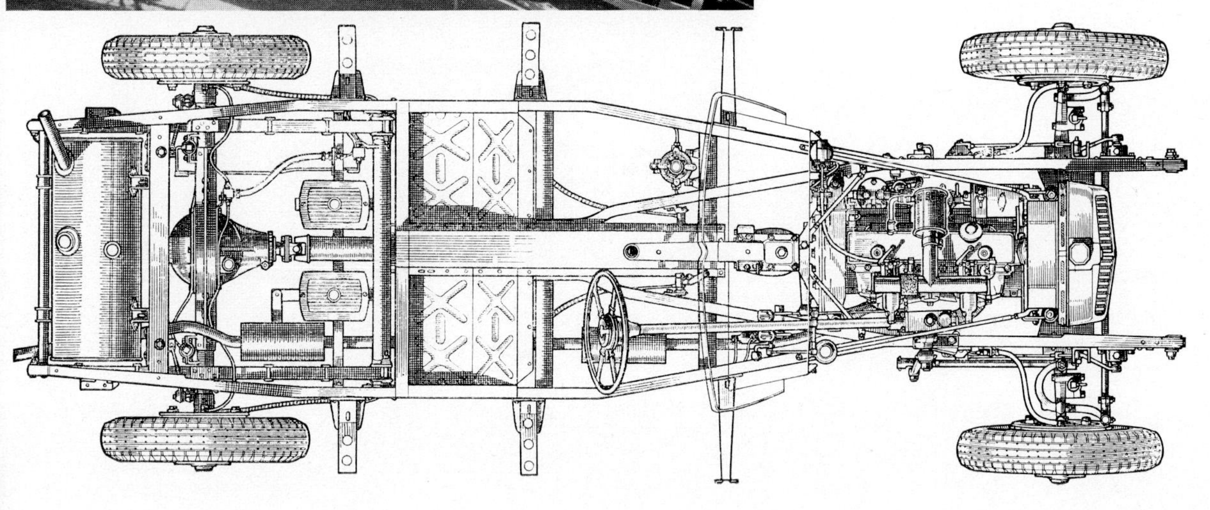

From any angle the SA saloon was good looking, even if sideways vision was a little restricted. The photo above is of a prototype, none were sold with bolt on wheels.

QUEEN OF GLEN ALBYN
QUEEN OF GLEN ALBYN

CWL 304

BJB 409

The drop-head Tickford Coupe, built by Salmons of Newport Pagnall was another attractive SA model.

The rather rare Charlesworth-bodied tourer was a good looking car with hood down, with ample room for full sized people, unlike the earlier post-vintage open tourers. Also unlike these cars, handling was not adversely affected with rear seats inhabited!

Above: *A typically continental-bodied SA from Keller of Switzerland — one of the very few successful special bodied M.G's.*

Below: *A half-way stage towards the WA, which shows that even in the late '30's M.G's underwent considerable development.*

The $1\frac{1}{2}$-litre VA followed the design precedents set by its larger relative. It was an attractive car, with reasonable performance, but not up to the standards set by the open Magnette it replaced.

The open tourer (Above) *was the least handsome of the VA models, with the Tickford Coupe* (Below) *perhaps the best looking.*

The 2.6-litre WA was a large well equipped car. Note the war-time headlamp shades in the saloon above — the war killed the model, which was M.G's last large engined saloon.

Once again in the SVW ranges it was Salmons' Tickford Coupe which gave the most attractive variant. Rearward vision must have been restricted with either head up or down !

These detail shots of the Tickford Coupe display (Above) *the coupe-de-ville position for the hood,* (Right) *the comfortable rear seats and* (Below) *a reversion to octagonal instruments.*

Above: *A Swiss-built WA Coupe by Keller, with four doors. The hood looks very Mercedes! Other Swiss coachbuilders who produced bodies for the WA included Reinbolt and Christé.*

Below: *A one-off WA Sedanca Coupe by Salmons, with a profile which suggests the Bentleys of Silent Sports Car fame. The price would have been around £1,000 less!*

CHAPTER SEVEN

Midgets for Export

As soon as the Second World War was over production of M.G's was resumed at Abingdon. The result was one of the best known of M.G's — the TC Midget.

The basis of the new car was the pre-war TB, with very similar engine, gearbox and axles. The chassis incorporated rubber-bushed and shackled road springs in place of the old trunnions, and the body was wider. Otherwise it was the same motor car.

That it sold was not surprising. That a large number went to Commonwealth countries, particularly South Africa and Australia was also not surprising as many M.G's had been sold there before the war. What did create a surprise however was that the sales increased in the U.S.A., particularly after 1948. It was the TC which precipitated the craze in America for British sports cars.

By 1949 the age of the TC was showing and a replacement was quickly made by taking the Y-type chassis, which had already been tried with a four-seater body as related in the next chapter, shortening it by five inches and mounting an improved TC body.

The car retained the engine of the TC, but fitted with the Y-type camshaft which improved the power range, otherwise it was mechanically identical with the Y-type.

Sales of the car positively soared, three times the number of these being sold as of TC's, and most of them were exported to the U.S.A. in four years.

During those years the TD was progressively improved, and in 1950 a Mark II or competition version was marketed alongside the normal version. The Mark II TD is quite a rare car, having Stage II tuned engine, bucket seats and extra front shock absorbers.

In 1953 the TF was introduced to replace the TD, which caused considerable disappointment, for enthusiasts were expecting something more modern. Mechanically it was a TD, although the engine was up to Mark II specification. The bodywork was only slightly "smoothed". Performance was disappointing, as were sales.

For 1955 a 1500cc version of the TF was announced, and although performance was increased, sales hardly improved and it became obvious that the long expected modern M.G. was needed. It followed in the middle of that year thus ending an illustrious run of motor cars.

The TC was a nice car but behind its time. It was frankly not as nice to drive either as its predecessor or its successors, but it has a tremendous following all over the world. The TD was probably the best of the T-types and is amongst the best M.G. Midgets. The TF is a modified TD and its appeal is a matter of opinion. All of the T-types have very similar performance in terms of figures, but it was the way in which this was achieved, rather than sheer performance, which ensured their great popularity — which continues to the present day.

SPECIFICATIONS

	TC	*TD Mark I**	*TD Mark II*	*TF*	*TF 1500*
Bore x Stroke	66.5 x 90 mm	66.5 x 90 mm	66.5 x 90 mm	66.5 x 90 mm	72 x 90 mm
Capacity	1250 cc	1250 cc	1250 cc	1250 cc	1466 cc
Valve operation	All models, pushrod overhead valves.				
Power output	54.4 bhp	54.4 bhp	60 bhp	57 bhp	63 bhp
@ rpm	5200	5200	5500	5500	5500
Gearbox	All models, four-speed with synchromesh on 2, 3 and 4 gears.				
Brakes	Hydraulic	Hydraulic 2LS at front	Hydraulic 2LS at front	Hydraulic 2LS at front	Hydraulic 2LS at front
Drums (diameter)	9″	9″	9″	9″	9″
Numbers built	10,000	28,643	1,022	6,200	3,400
Body Styles	All cars two-seat open sports only.				

* The 'Mark I' was never so-called. There is confusion now raised by the use of type numbers 'TD1' and 'TD2'. These do not exist, except that the connotation denotes a change in the clutch and flywheel assemblies which rendered these parts non interchangeable. The Mark II engine has the prefix 'TD3' in its engine number. The Mark II was known in the U.S.A. as the TDC.

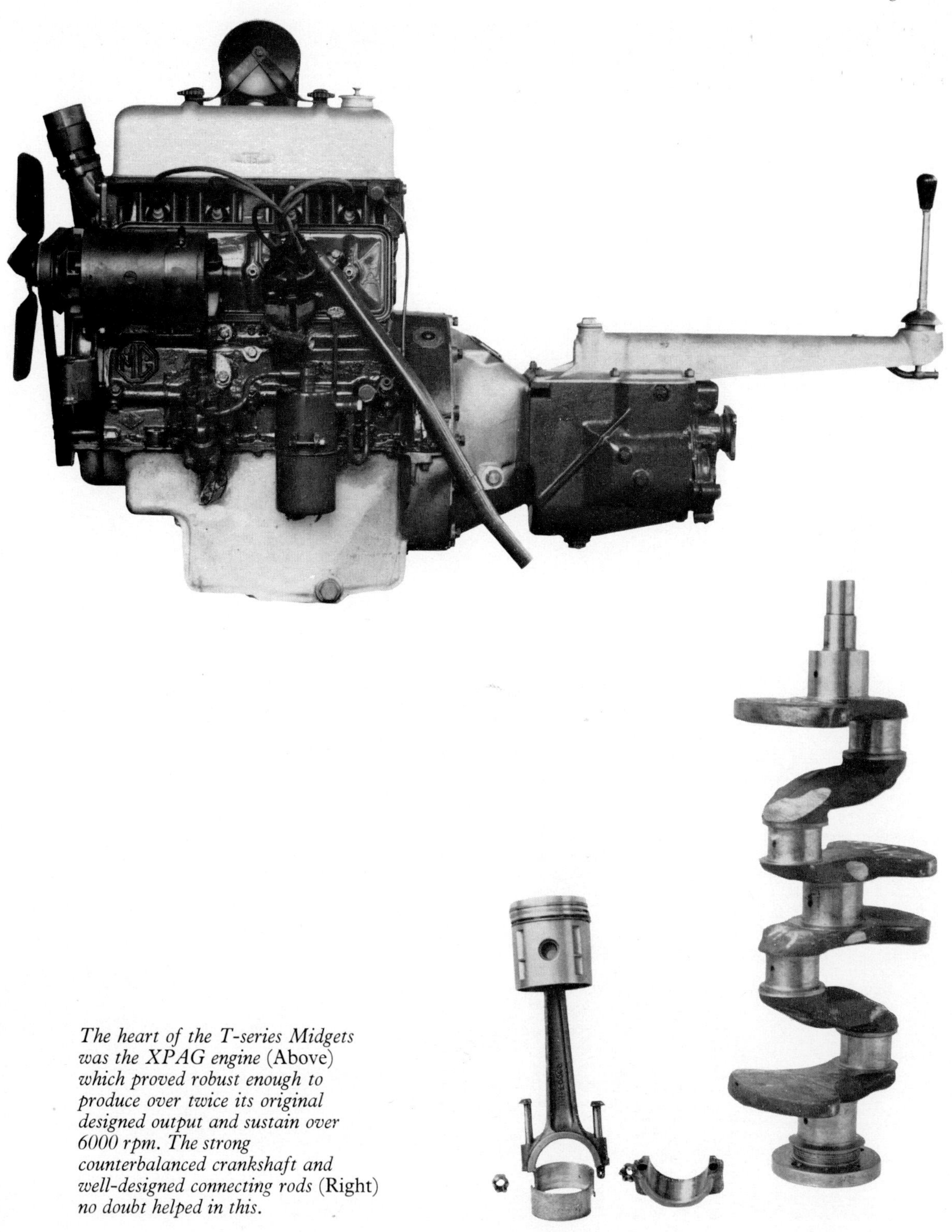

The heart of the T-series Midgets was the XPAG engine (Above) *which proved robust enough to produce over twice its original designed output and sustain over 6000 rpm. The strong counterbalanced crankshaft and well-designed connecting rods* (Right) *no doubt helped in this.*

The TC Midget here displays its obvious resemblance with the pre-war T-series cars. It ran for four years, as did the TA & TB, but sold over three times the number!

The TC had a comprehensive weather equipment (Above) *but was better suited to the race track* (Below). *Here an M.G. Car Club member performs at Silverstone in the mid-fifties, when the TC was already over ten years old. TC's are still raced with enthusiasm at Club events.*

The strong TD chassis is seen above. The front suspension (Right) *has featured in most M.G. sports cars since. Note the disc wheels which probably caused more criticism of the type than any other feature!*

Left: *The TC was the first M.G. to be exported to the U.S.A. in any number. This one poses outside a university library.*

The competition TD — the TD Mark II — differed from more mundane versions in respect of engine tune, front suspension modifications and bucket seats.

Above: *The hood of the TD was of similar type to the TC.* Left: *The interior was likewise similar, but the car was altogether more comfortable to drive.*

A special TD was prepared with all enveloping body for George Phillips to drive at Le Mans. It proved very fast, but the engine failed after three hours. The MGA was a direct development of this car.

Wire wheels were available as an option on the TD, but very few cars were originally so equipped. This one is a later modification.

The TD proved as successful in competition as was its predecessor: this one is a Mark II competing at a hill climb in Kenya.

That the TF chassis was directly related to that of the TD can be seen from these photographs, and that on Page 147. Note that the radiator grille is now carrying a sham cap, and covering a pressurised cooling system.

The TF was a "smoothed out" TD, and although much admired now was not regarded with enthusiasm when new.

Above: *The TF was available with wire wheels — this is a LHD example for export.*

Below: *Present General Secretary of the M.G. Car Club, Gordon Cobban, raced this TF in the mid-fifties with considerable success.*

CHAPTER EIGHT

Post War Saloons

The old M-type M.G. was derived from a rather unpromising saloon car. The current larger M.G. sports range was also developed from a saloon car, but in this case it was a car which had originally carried the proud octagon: the $1\frac{1}{4}$ litre Y-series.

Work on the Y-type series of saloons had commenced in 1939, and while the bodywork was very similar to the Morris and Wolseley 8 models, the chassis was something quite different. The car was finally introduced in 1947.

The frame was of box section, and underslung at the rear—rear suspension being by leaf springs. The front suspension was independent. The lessons of the R-type were not used, the torsion bar spring not appearing on an M.G. until 1967, wishbones and coil springs being the suspension medium. The upper wishbone doubled as the shock-absorber arm, the lower being fabricated from pressings.

The result was an immensely robust chassis, which formed the basis of the TD and TF sports range, and has continued to appear in modified form in the MGA and MGB series cars.

The engine used in the Y-type was a detuned version of the XPAG unit, having single carburetter, different valve timing and lower compression ratio. The gearbox was a four-speed synchromesh unit, which became renowned for its positive change. The rear axle was of conventional M.G. pattern. Steering was by rack and pinion for the first time on an M.G.

The whole car was very well appointed and very much on the SVW style. It was well received by the press and praise was well deserved, for it was a delightful car to drive, if prone to oversteer. It subsequently enjoyed good sales both at home and abroad.

In 1948 a tourer version of this car was introduced, and apart from the body the only difference was the use of the untuned engine as fitted to the TC. This car was a full four-seater, but was not particularly pretty in contrast to the pre-war tourers, carrying rather a large bulk aft. Most of this model were exported, but a very few remained in the U.K. before production ceased in 1951.

In 1951 the saloon was replaced by the YB model, which had smaller wheels, a hypoid rear axle and a Panhard rod at the rear, all of which improved handling, and made one of the nicest saloons of the time. It is still regarded with great affection.

The YB was replaced in 1953 by the first of the postwar Magnettes. The introduction of these well appointed saloons was greeted with shouts of disapproval from those who considered themselves M.G. historians. "Perversion of the famous name" was the kindest of many rude comments, but these sages had forgotten that the first Magnette had been a saloon aimed at a very similar type of customer.

Times had changed however, and the market for a soundly designed and responsive saloon with sporting pretensions had increased and very soon the Z-series Magnettes out-sold all previous M.G. saloons built at Abingdon, added together, and was destined to be the last M.G. saloon to be built at the M.G. factory.

The monocoque body design caused raised eyebrows—this was still considered "new" in 1953. Front suspension was by wishbones and coil springs, but different from the Y-type.

The engine was a B.M.C. 'B' series unit fitted with twin carburetters and mated to a gearbox of similar origin. Rear axle was likewise from the newly formed combine.

The interior was exceptionally well appointed, with a heater as standard and like many M.G's before, offered all that so called luxury cars did at a very much lower price.

An automatic clutch became available in the Manumatic Magnette, but this version was not popular, since the automatic operation was found to be a shade too automatic at times!

A ZB version was introduced in 1956, with more power and detail improvements, and a duotone version in 1958, called the "Varitone", and these two models ran side-by-side until the following year.

The car which replaced the ZB was called the Mark III Magnette, and was a quite different vehicle. The only components it shared with its predecessor were the engine, gearbox and rear axle and the instruments.

Gone was the good handling—very soft front suspension and poor geometry coupled with the worst form of steering box ensured that. Gone were the smooth lines, the boxy body which shared quite a few panels with the current Austin A60/Morris Oxford saloon ranges shewed that the era of centrally "designed" M.G's had returned.

In 1962 the car was improved immeasurably, and the Mark IV Magnette did have a reasonable degree of handling. The engine was increased to 1622cc which improved performance and an automatic gearbox became available. Unfortunately the car suffered because of its predecessor, and it had to be admitted that the ZB did handle better, but on the other hand it was not as bad as the majority of contemporary saloons and should have been better liked than it was. The model finally went out of production in 1969 and was not replaced.

Back in 1962, along with the not particularly inspired Magnette, a revolutionary M.G. was offered for sale. Like the R-type it had all independent suspension, but unlike the R-type this car was a saloon.

The Issigonis-designed 1100 range of B.M.C. cars is perhaps too recent history to describe in detail. Its cross-wise mounted engine with integral gearbox and front wheel drive, hydrolastic suspension and very rigid body shell appeared in various guises—for many years the best selling car in the United Kingdom, although not only in M.G. form!

In 1967 a 1275cc engine was offered making the model the 1300 and an automatic four-speed gearbox was introduced in association with a single carburetter engine. In 1969 only a two-door form was available, which ran until 1971 when the model was replaced by the Austin 1300 G.T.

Oddly enough many people mourned the passing of this the last M.G. saloon to date—for it displayed all the qualities of the best M.G's—it had good performance, was well appointed, handled impeccably, in short it was a good car.

SPECIFICATIONS

	YA/YB	*YT*	*ZA/ZB*	*Mk III*	*Mk IV*	*1100*	*1300*
Bore x Stroke	66.5 x 90 mm	66.5 x 90 mm	73 x 88.9 mm	73 x 88.9 mm	76.2 x 88.9 mm	64.6 x 83.7 mm	70.6 x 81.3 mm
Capacity	1250cc	1250cc	1489cc	1489cc	1622cc	1098cc	1275cc
Valve operation			All models: pushrod operated overhead valves.				
Approx. power output	46	54	ZA60 ZB68	66.5	68	55	70*
@ r.p.m.	4800	5200	ZA4600 ZB5250	5200	5000	5500	6000
Gearbox	4 speed Synchro on 2, 3, 4	4 speed Synchro on 2, 3, 4	4 speed Synchro on 2, 3, 4	4 speed Synchro on 2, 3, 4	4 speed Synchro on 2, 3, 4 or 3 speed automatic	4 speed Synchro on 2, 3, 4	4 speed All synchro** or 4 speed automatic
Brakes	Hydraulic 2LS on YB	Hydraulic	Hydraulic 2LS	Hydraulic 2LS	Hydraulic 2LS	Hydraulic, disc front, drum rear	Hydraulic, disc front, drum rear
Drums (diam.)	9″	9″	10″	9″	9″		
Number built	YA 6158 YB 1301	877	ZA 12754 ZB 23846	15676	13738	116827	26240
Body types	4 door saloon	4 seat tourer	4 door saloon	4 door saloon	4 door saloon	4 door saloon 2 door saloon (USA market only)	4 door saloon 2 door saloon

* Models fitted with automatic gearbox had a single carburetter engine at 60 b.h.p. at 5500 r.p.m.
** A few early 1300 models were built with gearboxes having synchromesh on the top three ratios only, and were called the "M.G. 1275".

The YA saloon was the first post-war M.G. saloon, from which the later T-type were derived. It set high standards of comfort, and offered good performance and handling. Note the octagonal instruments again!

The tourer version of the Y type, the YT, was not as handsome as the pre-war VA, but it was much higher and offered better performance from a smaller engine. Most of these cars were exported.

Above and Opposite: *The Magnette in its original ZA form. Received with mixed feelings it soon sold well and ran for nearly six years in various forms.*

Below: *The ZB which replaced it was only slightly refined, but is regarded as a far superior car.*

The ZB Magnette in (Above) *standard and form* (Below) *Varitone form, in which the two tone colour scheme was revived: it also improved rearward vision. The controls* (Left) *betrayed obvious M.G. ancestry.*

The Mark III (Above) *and Mark IV* (Right & Below) *was a car which few liked either from the aesthetic or performance point of view. The Mark IV was by far the better car, but its rather too obvious BMC ancestry was too much for the M.G. enthusiast.*

The M.G. 1100 was a success in spite of its ancestry! No doubt the excellent handling properties helped.

The 1100 was superceded in 1967 by the more powerful and better appointed 1300.

A special two-door version of the 1100 was sold in the USA, although complaints from users affected M.G. Sports Car sales for a time, and this was replaced by the Austin America in 1967.

In the final years of the 1300 only the two-door version was available. This is the last M.G. saloon to date, and probably offered the best performance of them all. Production ceased in 1971.

Specialist body builders were still trying their hands at improving the breed in the mid-sixties. This offering was a one-off by Douglas Wilson-Spratt.

CHAPTER NINE

Modern ABC

Firstly let it be said that the heading is wrong. The replacement of the TF Midget in 1955 was the MGA series, the 'A' type you will recall being the 18/80 Mark II.

The MGA signalled a new era in M.G. history. The car was a highly developed form of the TD, and had been completed some two years before it was actually introduced as a design exercise. The delay allowed the use of a developed form of the B series engine with Weslake modified cylinder head, and the resulting car was offered for sale shortly after its debut in the 1955 Le Mans race.

The new body was a success right from the start, and the fact that the handling was in the highest category of the time meant that the MGA was received with enthusiasm even by some of the most hardened M.G. enthusiasts.

A hardtop Coupe version became available in 1956 another attempt at producing a "G.T."style of car in the steps of pioneering pre-war Continental and Airline Coupes.

Progressively improved by use of disc brakes and larger engine the MGA outsold all other sports models added together.

There was even an ultra high performance version offered when in 1957 the MGA Twin Cam was introduced. This boasted a twin overhead camshaft engine, close ratio gearbox, four wheel disc brakes, centre lock disc wheels, and a truly superb performance for its size. Unfortunately, it suffered like the pre-war o.h.c. M.G's. in that it needed understanding hands to extract the best from it—and regrettably there are few people in the retail garage trade who are willing to spend the time necessary—and few customers prepared to pay for their time. The Twin-Cam was therefore killed off in 1959, and enjoys now a reverence equal to the earlier cars.

In 1962, just after the 100,000th MGA had been announced, the MGB was introduced to replace it. Powered by an increased capacity B-series engine fitted to a monocoque body, it is not generally appreciated how similar these two cars are mechanically. The MGB however was a modernised car and bore strong external family resemblance to the recently introduced Midget.

Overdrive became available in 1963 as an optional extra, and through the years the MGB has become progressively improved to maintain its position as the best value for money on the sports car market. It was supplemented in 1965 by the G.T. version, and these two cars have sold nearly 300,000 at the time of writing, not only outselling the previous total Abingdon-built M.G. production, but easily outselling each year all other sports cars.

In 1967 a six-cylinder MGC was introduced which shared a similar styled body to the MGB both open and G.T. forms but the suspension was by torsion bars at the front. Very few components in fact are interchangeable with the four-cylinder car, which probably contributed to the car's short life. The engine was a new design for the large BMC saloon cars, but in MGC form lacked the low speed torque expected of a three litre unit. On the other hand the gearbox was there to be used, and an MGC is probably the fastest M.G. so far built, apart from the record breakers. It was a maligned car in its time, and is now becoming a sought after vehicle.

SPECIFICATIONS

	MGA 1500	*MGA 1600*	*MGA 1600† Mk II*	*MGA Twin Cam*	*MGB Mk I. II, III**	*MGC*
Bore x stroke	73 x 88.9 mm	75.4 x 88.9 mm	76.2 x 88.9 mm	75.4 x 88.9 mm	80.3 x 88.9 mm	83.4 x 88.9 mm
Capacity	1489cc	1588cc	1622cc	1588cc	1789cc	2912cc
Valve operation	All models: pushrod operated overhead valves					
Power output	68**	80	93	108	95‡	145
@ r.p.m.	5500	5600	5500	6700	5400	5250
Gearbox	4 speed Synchro on 2, 3, 4	4 speed Synchro on 2, 3, 4	4 speed Synchro on 2, 3, 4	4 speed Synchro on 2, 3, 4	Mk I: 4 speed Synchro on 2, 3, 4 Mk II, III: 4 speed all synchro *or* 3 speed automatic	4 speed all synchro *or* 3 speed automatic
Brake system	Hydraulic, disc brakes at front for all models except early MGA which had drums all round, and Twin Cam which had a four wheel disc system. MGC had servo-assisted system as standard.					
Number built	58750	31501	8719	2111	Still in production 1972	8999
Body Types	2 seat tourer	2 seat tourer 2 seat coupe	2 seat tourer 2 seat coupe	2 seat tourer 2 seat coupe	2 seat tourer 2 seat G.T.	2 seat tourer 2 seat G.T.

* Mk I 1962-67, Mk II 1967-71, Mk III 1971 to date.
** Later increased to 72 bhp @ 5500 r.p.m.
† A small number of "MGA 1600 Mk II de Luxe" were built using the 1622cc engine in a Twin Cam chassis.
‡ This is the officially quoted figure for all types of engine and may be regarded as a production average.

The MGA was the last M.G. to have a separate chassis. Front suspension was similar to that of the TF while the engine and transmission were from the Magnette. Very few modifications were necessary to this car to make it one of the best production sports cars of its time.

The MGA had clean lines, and from its inception, was available with either wire wheels (above) *or pressed steel disc wheels* (below).

A Factory fitted hardtop was available for the first time on an M.G., but was obviously an accessory (above). *The fixed-head coupe* (below) *was a more attractive car.*

The MGA Twin Cam was the fastest production version of the model, available in Coupe (above) *and open* (below) *forms. The engine filled the available bonnet space* (left) *which rendered servicing difficult.*

The MGA Mark II 1600 had a revised grille (above) *and the model was current when the hundred-thousandth MGA left the production line* (below) *in 1961. This milestone celebrated a hitherto unprecedented mark in sports car history.*

The MGB appeared to be a scaled-up Midget. Its monocoque body certainly looked like the Midget, but had a personality of its own. The car proves popular in Club racing—the one below being one of the earliest production cars, only very slightly modified from standard.

(Above) *An early MGB displays its distinctive front view.*
(Below) *Successive American Safety Regulations have resulted in a special model for that market. This is a 1971 model fitted with Factory hardtop.*

The MGB G.T. was introduced in 1965 and still proves a most popular car of its type (above and left) *a 1965 model.* (Below) *a 1972 model with recessed front grille.*

(Above) *An automatic gearbox was offered on the MGB from 1967 as an option—here is the selector, reminiscent of the pre-selector quadrant of the K Magnettes.*
(Right) *Headlamp cowls have been offered by British Leyland Special Tuning and other suppliers.*
(Below) *The 1973-model MGB G.T. showing the revised grille.*

The MGC looked similar to the MGB, and this may not have helped it to sell. It was, in fact, considerably different, apart from the engine (left), *having larger wheels, torsion-bar front suspension and many other detail differences.*

CHAPTER TEN

Modern Midgets

When, in 1957, the Austin-Healey Sprite was announced there were many enthusiasts who said that it should not have borne that name. Most of these were Riley men who did not like the thought of one of their model names being used on a car of another make. I agreed with those who thought the car was wrongly named, but for a different reason. B.M.C., the owners of both the marques mentioned, already had in their fold a sports car which sold without effort — why introduce a brand new one? A further rebuke to M.G. was the fact that the new car was built at Abingdon.

In the event the Sprite sold well, but how much better it would have sold if called an M.G. Midget was not put to the test until 1961, shortly after the Sprite Mark II was announced. The M.G. Midget was one of these cars with a better radiator grille! Both versions were designed and built at Abingdon.

Powered by a 948 cc engine it was the first under one-litre M.G. since the PB, and filled the gap left by that car very well. Performance was even much the same, although it was a more comfortable car to drive.

The suspension was by wishbones and coil springs at the front and quarter elliptic springs at the rear, a one-piece rear axle being retained. The bodywork was smart and smooth, and there was a reasonably sized luggage boot.

Shortly after introduction the power output was uprated which gave straight line performance more in keeping with a car of the 'sixties, and in 1962 the engine was increased in size to 1098 cc giving further improvements. This last increase in power was met by increased braking efficiency for disc brakes were fitted at the front.

In 1964 the Mark II Midget was introduced, which featured wind-up windows, bringing the specification into line with that of the MGB. Power was increased further making it a near 100 mph performer. Rear suspension was modified to semi-elliptic springs to ensure handling remained of the highest order with the increased performance.

In 1966 a 1275 cc engine was fitted and this, coupled with a higher back axle ratio, and an improved hood was the Mark III, which continues though with minor modifications.

In 1967 the United States of America required imported motor cars to be in compliance with safety and exhaust emission regulations, and so appeared the first of the annual model changes which have occurred since, which is a reversion to the annual model change policy of the 1920's era.

In 1964 three special coupé Midgets were built for racing purposes, two of which were run by Dick Jacobs and one by John Milne. The former featured for a number of years in sports and GT events ensuring that the M.G. Midget had competition success of similar stature to that enjoyed by earlier models.

Through the years the Midget has been improved progressively which has ensured that it carried on the traditions of "Safety Fast". It certainly offers, like all Midgets before, a vehicle which is practical and yet enjoyable to drive, and which can be entered in club motor sporting events with a minimum of modification. The formula is so successful that well over 100,000 have been built to date and production shows little sign of slowing down.

SPECIFICATIONS

	Mark I *GAN 1*	*Mark I* *GAN 2*	*Mark II* *GAN 3*	*Mark III* *GAN 4 and 5*
Bore x Stroke	62.9 x 76.2 mm	64.6 x 83.7 mm	64.6 x 83.7 mm	70.6 x 81.3 mm
Capacity	948 cc	1098 cc	1098 cc	1275 cc
Valve operation	All models: pushrod overhead valve.			
Power output	46.4 bhp*	55 bhp	59 bhp	65 bhp
@ rpm	5500	5500	5750	6000
Gearbox	All models: four-speed with synchromesh on 2, 3 and 4.			
Brakes	Hydraulic, 2LS at front	Hydraulic, disc at front	Hydraulic, disc at front	Hydraulic, disc at front
Number built	16,080	9,601	26,601	Still in production
Body Style	All models: two-seater open tourer.			

* Later increased to 50 bhp at 5500 rpm.

The 948cc Midget was an attractive little car bringing less-than-one-litre motoring back for M.G. enthusiasts for the first time since 1936.
(Below) *It progressively grew up however gaining an 1100cc engine and wind-up windows in the Mark II form of 1963.*

In Mark III form the engine increased still further to 1275cc and a smart and practical foldaway hood was adopted.

The instrument panel of the Midget has not changed much, the home market version still being essentially the same as the Mark I, although rocker switches are now used.

The U.S.A. version has an energy absorbing surface ahead of the driver and most recent cars have had a glove box mounted below.

The 1971 Midget (above) *had distinctive pattern wheels, which were replaced in 1972 by Rostyle type similar to those fitted to the MGB* (below). *The grille sports an octagonal badge, but is not as distinctive as that of earlier Midgets.*

CHAPTER ELEVEN

Magic Achievements

Since 1923 M.G.s have successfully appeared in competitions of all types, ranging from reliability trials and driving tests to racing and record breaking.

To give a faithful record of over forty years' competitions is just not possible in this book, and this chapter seeks only to provide some evidence that M.G's not only used to take part in events, but still do so.

Perhaps the most renowned era of M.G. participation was that in the nine years prior to the Second World War, when M.G. almost annexed the 750 cc and 1100 cc classes as its own. By 1935 it had become a matter of deciding which M.G. would win the awards rather than which *marque!*

After retirement from racing car manufacture in 1935, M.G's continued to be successful with modified older cars and, more recently, modified production models. Single-seater K3's and Q-types have continued to compete with success right up to the present time, although standard cars have now largely been relegated to museums, which is a pity.

Two of the best known cars of this period are those which inspired the title of this book, namely Magic Midget, the first 750 cc car to achieve two miles a minute, and Magic Magnette, which was to become both a successful racing and record breaking car. In the latter field it was the first car to exceed 200 mph in *both* the 1100 and 1500 cc classes, *and* the first 750 cc car to exceed three miles a minute. It also took a great number of other records before being retired in 1952.

Mention must also be made here of an M.G. being the first 750 cc car to exceed 100 mph in 1930, and another being the first 1500 cc car to exceed four miles a minute in 1957, and the first 2-litre car to exceed the same mark and 250 mph in 1959. The wide range of M.G. achievements in record breaking is unparalleled.

MGB's and Midgets were used in production car events until 1969, as did the TC's TD's and MGA's before them. All of these cars are regularly seen at minor club events in the U.K. to the present time, modified Midgets offering a relatively cheap introduction to motor sport at competitive speeds.

Reliability trials were the preserve of M.G's in the latter half of the 'thirties, the M.G. Car Club teams named the "Cream Crackers" and "Three Musketeers" being best known, although many other teams were formed which ensured M.G. cars were always featured in the results.

In rallies M.G's were less successful, although they have taken part in these events since 1929 through to the present time. MGA's and Z Magnettes were probably more successful in this field than any other M.G. type.

I hope you enjoy this selection in which a balance of various eras has been sought, as well as the reproduction of a few more unusual photographs.

The first known racing success of an M.G. car. Cires driving his 1927 14/40 at the horse race track of San Martin near Buenos Aires.

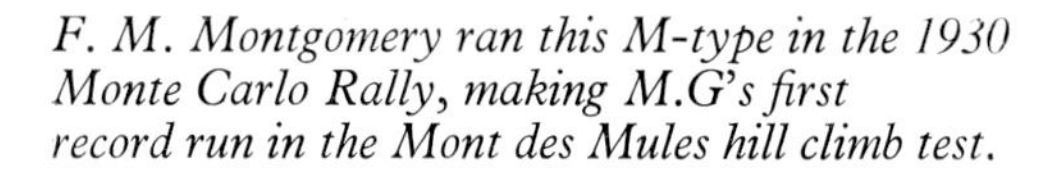

F. M. Montgomery ran this M-type in the 1930 Monte Carlo Rally, making M.G's first record run in the Mont des Mules hill climb test.

Two specially prepared M-types based on the 12/12 model were run at Le Mans in 1930. This one was driven by R. C. Murton-Neale and Jack Hicks, retiring after 17 hours running.

M.G's first significant racing victory was in the 1931 J.C.C. Double Twelve race at Brooklands. Here three of the successful cars pose with the mechanics in the cockpits and the rest of the M.G. personnel outside the office block at Abingdon.

EX 120 being started up at Pendine, George Eyston is driving, Reg Jackson pushing at the offside rear wheel. E. A. D. Eldrigde is at the right of the group. At Montlhery this car subsequently achieved the first 100 mph in the 750 cc class in 1930.

A C-type at Abingdon, Cyril Paul behind the wheel, talking to Goldie Gardner (Centre) *and Eddie Hall.*

C-types are still occasionally seen racing, this one is at Silverstone driven by Bob Hudson.

Magic Midget — George Eyston up! This car and driver successfully broke the Class H 2 miles-per-minute record in 1932.

The K3 prototype (Left) *which was driven by F. M. Montgomery in the 1933 Monte Carlo Rally, breaking the class record in the Mont des Mules. This same car won the first race for a K3 driven by R. T. Horton at Donnington, but two weeks later two K3's won the 1100 cc class and the Team Award in the Mille Miglia* (Below).

Nuvolari won the 1933 TT in a K3. Above: *He is seen during the race and* (Left) *after, with Alec Hounslow, his riding mechanic, and Reg Jackson who was responsible for the preparation of the car.*

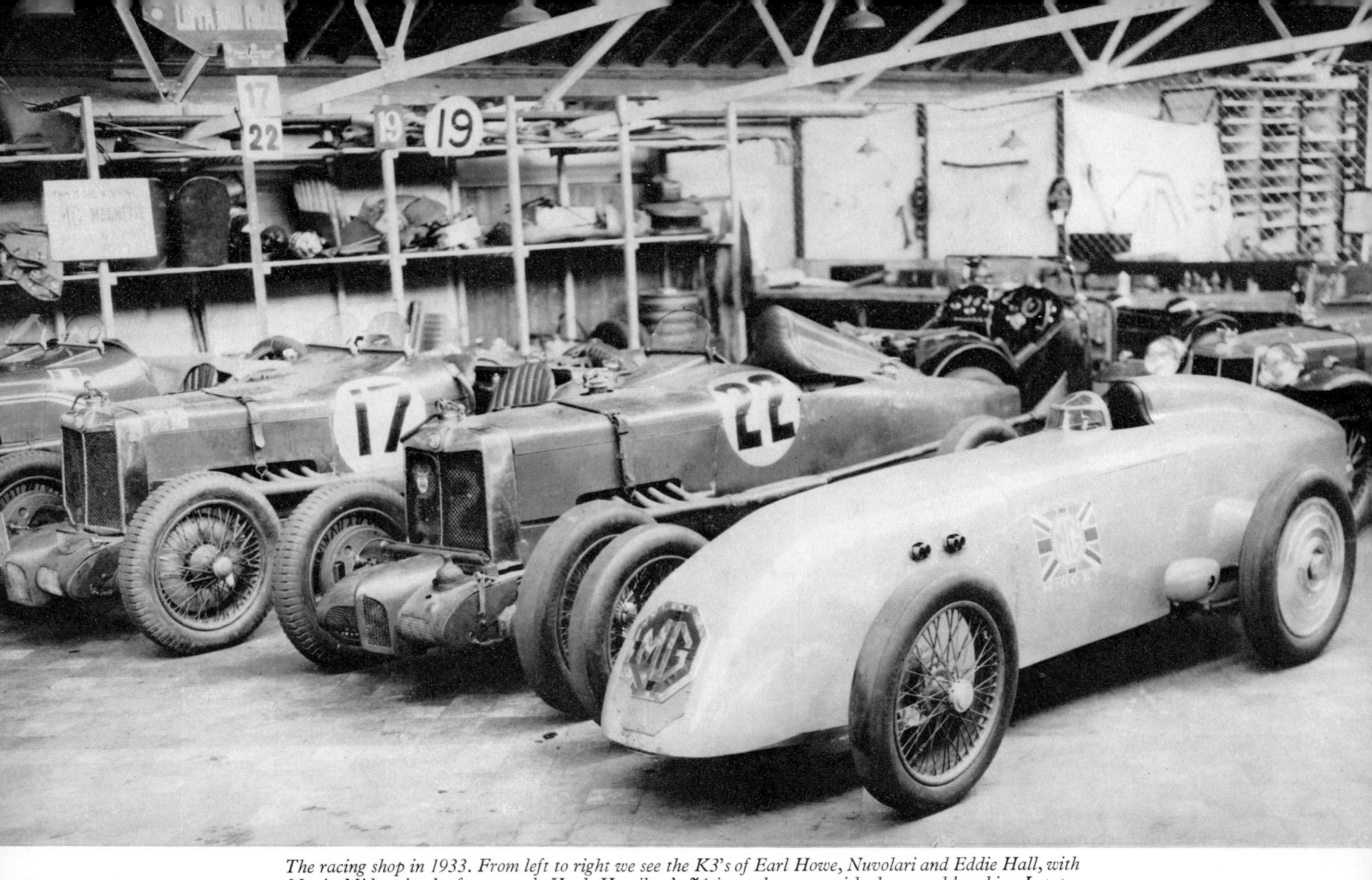

The racing shop in 1933. From left to right we see the K3's of Earl Howe, Nuvolari and Eddie Hall, with Magic Midget in the foreground. Hugh Hamilton's J4 is at the rear, with the record breaking L-type.

Goldie Gardner at Brooklands in his first K3 which was subsequently run by J. H. T. Smith with great success.

Below: *Jacques Menier ran this K3 during 1934/5, Maillard Brune and Druck winning the two-litre class at the 1935 Le Mans race.*

The success of the racing o.h.c. M.G. was due solely to careful preparation. Ted Starkie here puts the finishing touches to a K3 unit, while Jock Routledge works on a J4 unit.

The most famous K3 of all: "Magic Magnette". Painted in cream and brown stripes it was more familiarly called the "Humbug". More serious minded engineers referred to it as EX135. The transmission line was set at 6° to the centre line allowing the driver to sit lower than in a standard car.

A J4 at Craigantlet in 1938, driven here by E. R. Robb. The engine of this car was reputed to run at 9000 rpm!

J. C. Elwes' J4 at a pre-war Crystal Palace meeting.

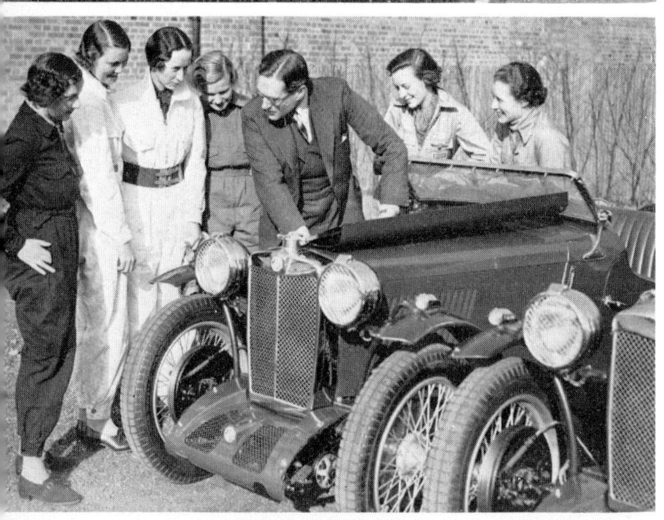

The celebrated "Dancing Daughters" team which George Eyston managed at the 1935 Le Mans race. Left to right are Betty Skinner, Barbara Eaton, Joan Richmond, Margaret Allen, George Eyston, Doreen Evans, Margaret Simpson. The car is a PA.

This supercharged NA was run in the 1935 Monte Carlo Rally by journalist Humfrey Symons and M.G. mechanic Freddie Kindell. All set to win the event, Symons succeeded in crashing during the final driving test, but took second place in the Concours! It is still raced by the author.

The first event for the NE, the new un-supercharged car built for the TT was the 1934 J.C.C. Relay Race, the cars being placed 3rd, driven by a team of ladies. Left to right are Irene Schwendler, Margaret Allen and Doreen Evans.

After their success in the 1934 event the NE's ran again in the 1935 event, driven by Dick Seaman (Left) *Kenneth Evans* (Centre) *and his elder brother Dennis. The highest place achieved was Seaman, 10th.*

Rebodied, and renamed the "Three Musketeers", the NE's won the Welsh Rally in 1935, driven by (Left to right) Sam Nash, Freddie Kindell and Lewis Welch.

The "Cream Crackers" and "Three Musketeers" teams for 1935 in line astern: MacDermid, Bastock, Toulmin, Nash, Kindell and Welch. The cars are PA's and NE's.

George Harvey-Noble's special bodied Q-type (Left) *which forever holds the Class H lap record on Brooklands Outer Circuit at 122.4 mph, set in 1937.*

Below: *An unusual picture of an R-type at Brooklands, with George Eyston at the wheel. H. N. Charles, the designer, admires his handiwork with Cecil Cousins.*

Above: *the 1936 Cream Cracker's team of supercharged PB's before the start of the Team Trial at Buxton.*

Right: *R. A. MacDermid with one of the 1938 Musketeer's TA's at New Mill during the Lands End Trial.*
Below: *A pre-war M.G. Car Club Abingdon trial. Dickie Green prepares to start in this blown PB.*

EX 135 in its best known form, with Railton-designed body. Left: *Reg Jackson and Syd Enever discuss points before a run with the 750 cc engine in 1947.*

Below: *A. F. Rivers Fletcher, who became associated with M.G's at Monaco Engineering, in Duke Wooley's TB prepared for the 1939 TT race which was never held.*

Even the SVW's took part in competition — this is the concours section of an M.G. Car Club rally.

The TC special which George Phillips ran at Le Mans in 1950.

TC's proved very popular in all forms of competition after the war — this one is at the Rest and be Thankful Hill Climb.

Y-types took part in saloon car racing in the early 1950's, but this one belonging to Dick Bean, and driven by Goldie Gardner, achieved 104.7 mph in 1951. It was supercharged but otherwise standard.

Dick Jacobs has been associated with M.G. racing from 1947 to the present time. Here he is with a TD/TF based special which he built in 1953.

The mechanics and designer with the 1955 Le Mans entries — prototype MGA's. They are (Left to right) Harold Wiggins, 'Dick' Whittington, Den Green, Alec Hounslow, Syd Enever, Jim Cox, Cliff Bray and Gerald Wiffen.

EX135 in its final form with supercharged XPAG engine fitted, in which form it exceeded 200 mph, but was not quite fast enough to beat the Class F speeds set pre-war with the six-cylinder unit.

EX181: the M.G. which exceeded 4 miles per minute (Class F) in 1957 and 250 mph (Class E) in 1959, driven by Stirling Moss and Phil Hill respectively.

Above: *The MGA Twin Cam team which ran at Sebring in 1959, and two of which finished 2nd and 3rd in their class.*

The Marathon de la Route MGB of 1966, which won the 84 hour event outright, driven by Andrew Hedges and Julian Vernaeve.

One of the two special bodied Midget Coupés which were run firstly by Dick Jacobs then by B.M.C. Competitions until 1967, with considerable success. Both cars exist in their original form, and are still raced.

Timo Makinen and John Rhodes drove this MGB at Sebring in 1967, finishing 3rd in class.

Right: *This alloy bodied MGB G.T. was run at Sebring in 1968 by Gary Rodriguez and Dick McDaniels, finishing 6th in the G.T. category.*
Below: *The successful B.M.C. line up for the 1968 Sebring race. (Left to Right) Class winning Sprite prototype (Garton/Baker), the MGB G.T., pictured above, a Midget (Truitt/Canfield) which won its class and the Group IV category, and MGB (Hedges/Hopkirk) which won its class, and was 10th overall.*

Competition for M.G's is kept alive through the M.G. Car Club, which organises concours for old cars (Above) *and races for newer ones* (Below) *— and races for old cars and concours for new ones! The picture above was taken at Beaulieu and that below at Brands Hatch in 1972.*

CHAPTER TWELVE

Magic Methods

The photographs which follow are a collection which give some idea of pre-war operations, and a few cars which could not otherwise be classified.

Unfortunately the pictures left out are just as interesting as these here and in many ways this was the most difficult selection to make.

What we have attempted in this chapter is to show something of production methods before the war, and one or two cars which could not be readily classified.

M.G's were first built in a mews garage in Oxford, bodies being built by Raworths amongst others. In 1925 production moved to the Osberton Radiators Works off the Banbury Road, and in 1927 to the first exclusive M.G. factory in Edmund Road, Cowley. It was at this time that the M.G. Car Co., was first formed, and M.G. first accepted their own guarantee claims.

The move to Abingdon took place in 1930, when the limited company was first incorporated, and where M.G's have been built ever since — with the exception of saloons after 1959.

Other marques have been built at Abingdon: all Rileys built after the war until the demise of the Pathfinder, the Morris Minor vans and Travellers for a period and then the Austin-Healey Sports cars until their demise in 1971.

Factory methods have not changed much although such modern adjuncts to production as rolling roads and tuning aids are now used. Also it is not generally known that it was at M.G. that the world's first facility for testing production cars in large numbers for compliance with exhaust emission laws of the U.S.A. was inaugurated in 1967.

M.G. sports cars have been built at the Pavlova works for over forty years, building a reputation which is unrivalled anywhere in the world, and the envy of all competitors.

Above: *One of Morris Garages premises — at Merton Street.*
Centre: *A posed shot showing the collection of a 14/40 at Edmund Road.*
Below: *A Morris Commercial lorry used by Morris Garages — not an M.G. model!*

Top: *The Service Bay at Edmund Road.*
Above: *One of the bays at the new Abingdon factory early in 1930. Cecil Cousins stands in the foreground.*
Right: *The chassis finishing shop at Edmund Road.*
Below: *Rows of L-types at Abingdon, during late 1933.*

A line of chassis outsid: Edmund Road factory about to be driven to Coventry for fitting of bodies by Carbodies Limited.

Sir William Morris (later Lord Nuffield) visits the 18/80 production lines at Abingdon in 1930.

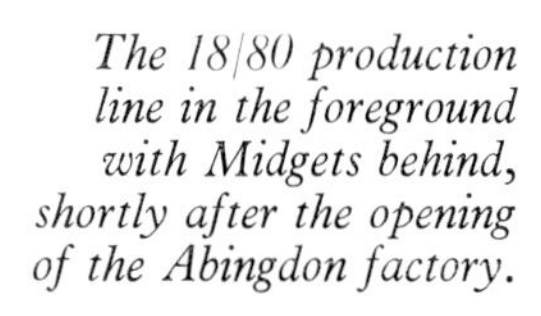

The 18/80 production line in the foreground with Midgets behind, shortly after the opening of the Abingdon factory.

Engines were fitted to the Midget in the same way in 1930 as in the 1970's.

The body drop at Abingdon: another M-type becomes a car . . . . wonder if this one still exists?

Bodies arriving at Abingdon, three to a crate — just £19.50 worth.

Above: *A nice showroom display at Jarvis, with their own versions of the Midget in the foreground.*
Centre: *A row of J-type radiators.*
Below: *An L-type chassis having its brakes adjusted and tested.*

Some Abingdon specials! The SA above started life as BRM 70, which Tommy & Elsie Wisdom drove in the 1937 Mille Miglia, but crashed. The tractor below served through the war years as a general hack — the M.G. special of all time! Syd Enever poses 2nd from right in centre picture!

M.G's have found favour with police forces right from the early 1930s. The TA and VA were the first to be offered in Police Specification, and many subsequent models have been built since.

BRITISH CARS' TRIUMPH IN 1,000 MILE RACE

WINNER'S OWN STORY OF TENSE 18-HOUR BATTLE

CAPT. EYSTON & EARL HOWE BEAT ALL RIVALS

"BABY" M.G. MAGNETTES' NEW COURSE RECORDS

SECRET NEW 130-m.p.h. BRITISH CAR

BY THOMAS H. WISDOM

A NEW British car is to appear in Britain's biggest motor-race of the year, the International Trophy, which is to be run at Brooklands on Jubilee Bank Holiday.

Designed and built in great secrecy during the past six months, the new racer is an M.G.—a small single-seater machine with an engine nominally rated at 8 horse-power, but which actually develops 120 horse-power.

It is fitted with independently sprung wheels, the first British racing car to be so equipped.

It is believed to be capable of over 130 miles an hour.

A team has been entered for the International Trophy, the drivers being Captain George Eyston, Norman Black and Wal Handley, a formidable combination.

Driving the new French Bugatti racers are the Hon. Brian Lewis, A. H. L. Eccles and C. E. C. Martin. Two Italian Maseratis are to be driven by Gino Rovere—who will have as his second driver Whitney Straight, the winner last year—and Guiseppe Fari ... the only foreign drivers in the ra...

Then there are the ... Romeos to be driven by ... worth and Dr. J. D. ... British E.R.A.s of ... "Tim" Rose-Richard... field; and Freddy ... Riley.

Already in the r... who returned to th... sational win on N... crash which woul... men's speed care... the winner of th...

CAR FIRM GIVES UP RACING

AFTER FAMOUS VICTORIES

It was announced last night that the M.G. Car Company, just taken over by Morris Motors, Ltd., will no longer race their cars.

This decision brings to a close one of the most remarkable sequences of victories ever known in motoring. Henceforward any new M.G. records will be achieved by private drivers working alone.

Since the creation of the M.G. company some ten years ago they have seen their little cars break records on more than 500 occasions, which include practically every world record possible for this size of car.

The baby car speed record, for instance, has been raised by M.G.s in repeated successes from about 70 to more than 130 m.p.h.